Revelations from Heaven's Doorway

by Marilyn Ryerson

Fire Wind™

Mansfield, PA

ISBN: 1-883906-40-7   Revelations from Heaven's Doorway (paperback)

Fire Wind
P.O. Box 506
Mansfield, PA 16933

(570) 662-7515
(800) 597-1123

http:/ /www.kingdompub.com
email = info@kingdompub.com

To the

Congregants

of

Northview Christian Life

and to

all those whose lives

have been touched

by

Tommy Paino III

Contents

Preface   7

Acknowledgments   9

Part 1

1. A Bitter Communion   13

2. Life Planner   21

3. I Have Learned   29

4. The Potter's House   37

5. Of Monks and Fruitcakes   45

6. Am I Alone?   53

Part 2

7. A Book is Born   63

8. The Remembering One   71

9. Undaunted Courage   85

10. Raising the Knife   93

11. To the Congregation   103

12. Beckoning to the Bridge   113

13. The Mystery of Healing 125

14. Trembling on Holy Ground 135

15. Good Friday 143

——————————— *Part 3* ———————————

16. Descending the Rope 155

17. Elijah Must Go 163

18. Life in a Hermitage 171

19. A Sequestered Path 179

20. The Deafening Silence 187

21. An Unkind Friend 195

22. Parting Words 203

23. The Storm 209

Epilogue 213

Notes 219

Works Cited 222

Preface

Tommy Paino had never written a book, at least not in the more traditional sense. Nevertheless, in a small Midwestern town north of Indianapolis there is a living book, a body of believers who, week after week, month after month, year after year, drank in the words of grace and encouragement spoken by Thomas Paino III in his Sunday sermons. Each child, each woman, and each man is a living page in Tommy's book, testifying to the love of God in Christ as expressed in the community of Northview Christian Life in Carmel, Indiana.

This book is but a synopsis of the words written on the pages of the hearts of those who are a part of this body of believers. It contains the words spoken by Tommy directly to me during the last months of his journey down a dark and narrow path through a sweeping, unrelenting storm of ALS, amyotrophic lateral sclerosis, more commonly known as Lou Gehrig's Disease.

Acknowledgments

Writing a book is not a gift that a writer gives to others, but rather it is a gift that others give to the writer. The support of the staff and congregation of Northview Christian Life Church has helped to make this book possible. Thank you. A great debt of thanks is also due my administrative assistant, Mary Kaye Wells, whose gentle pruning of my schedule secured the time needed to write this book. To Peggy Pickering, who painstakingly typed two years of sermons and notes—what can I say? Without your dedication, I would still be on page one. I am also greatly indebted to all of you who have read draft after draft of this manuscript. Your feedback has shaped my writing, this story, and me. Without the emotional and spiritual support of family and friends, this project would not have come to pass. Bouquets to all of you for cheering me on. And to you, Sandy Paino, I am deeply indebted. Your courage encouraged me. Your faithfulness increased my faith. Your love for God and Tommy has left me speechless.

Thank you

Marilyn S. Ryerson

Part 1

Who Am I? They also tell me,
I would step from my cell's confinement
calmly, cheerfully, firmly,
like a squire from his country-house.

— — — — — — — —

Who Am I? They also tell me
I would bear the days of misfortune
equably, smilingly, proudly,
like one accustomed to win.

Am I then really all that which other men tell of?
Or am I only what I know of myself,
restless and longing and sick, like a bird in a cage,
struggling for breath, as though hands were
compressing my throat.

— — — — — — — —

Who Am I?
They mock me, these lonely questions of mine.
Whoever I am, thou knowest, O God, I am thine.

Dietrich Bonhoeffer,
"Who Am I?"

Chapter 1
"A Bitter Communion"

> *I*f God has made your cup sweet,
>
> drink it with grace;
>
> if God has made it bitter,
>
> drink it in communion with Him.

Oswald Chambers,
My Utmost for His Highest

The story that I started to tell is not the story I have written. What began as a chronicle of the last months of a dying man, became a handbook on how to live by faith. Oh, the chapters of Tommy Paino's life remain the same, but in the writing of this book I have changed; and the story I have to tell has more to do with how to live than how to die.

In "real" time, that is time as we experience it in accordance with the Gregorian calendar, it all began in October of 1995. However, from an infinite-eternal perspective, God intruded into the veil of time and tapped Tommy Paino on the shoulder. It was no ordinary tap. It was the kind of tap that all of us goal-oriented, magical thinkers have prayed for, truly believing that if God tapped us on the shoulder and revealed His intent for our future, we would better serve the Infinite-Eternal in the here and now. On October 13th, 1995, the Infinite-Eternal did tap Tommy Paino on the shoulder, and when Tommy turned to look, he found a scroll rolled out in front of him. On it, written by the finger of God, was a time line for the rest of his life.

"Tommy, I just heard from one of the pastors that you are having some strange symptoms. Is there anything I can do for you?"

This was the first of thousands of questions that Tommy Paino would answer about his condition over the coming months. Friends and congregational members stopped him in the sanctuary, near the door to his office, at the grocery store, and on the street. No matter where Tommy went, he would meet someone who had heard about his condition. Most of these questions were born out of a real concern for his well-being as well as a deep need to understand how God would respond to a man whose message had always been one of faith in the midst of insurmountable obstacles. First there had been weakness in his right hand—and then in his left hand. What he had originally thought was carpal tunnel syndrome turned out to be something far more serious.

"Thank you for your concern, Jerry. Your continued prayers for me and my family are what I need most right now," Tommy responded with a smile.

What keeps us coming back to our faith in spite of doubt and sometimes in spite of pain? What keeps us believing in a good God when things around us appear so bleak? These were no longer theoretical questions for Tommy. Every day since the diagnosis Tommy's parents had made the drive across town to pray with him, and every day Tommy would receive a letter from his father with words of encouragement and faith.

Tommy came from a long line of believers. He had grown up in the church. His grandfather and his father were pastors. Tommy had also followed in their footsteps, and he, too, was a pastor. Faith in Jesus Christ in all things had been the mainstay of his message for almost twenty-five years. Now, after a lifetime of preaching, teaching, and believing, Tommy Paino's faith was about to be tested.

Tommy's thoughts fell on words from the Scripture that he had always loved. "'You do not want to leave too, do you?' Jesus asked the Twelve.

"Simon Peter answered him, 'Lord, to whom shall we go? You have the words of eternal life'" (John 6:67,68). At this moment Tommy needed the words of eternal life to wash over his soul and renew his faith in the face of unrelenting fear.

Only a week ago, sitting in a steel-gray upholstered chair in a small cubicle room of his doctor's office, Tommy had heard these words.

"Well, I must tell you that the diagnosis is not good. You have Lou Gehrig's disease," the doctor blurted out without looking up from her notes. Calmly and matter-of-factly, she continued. "That means that you can expect to live three to four more years. All your voluntary muscles will atrophy to total paralysis. When your chest muscles—which control the diaphragm's movement for breathing—atrophy, you will die of asphyxiation..."

Did the doctor not understand what she had just said? A torrent of conflicting emotions swept over him. Tommy's world had just turned upside down, and yet she didn't seem to notice. Words continued to flow from her mouth, her lips moved, but Tommy only heard the echo in his head, "Lou Gehrig's...Lou Gehrig's...Lou Gehrig's..."

His mind began to question. "What will happen to my family? What will happen to the church? Where is God in all of this?" Thoughts raced through his mind. He could feel the heat rising to the top of his bald head.

A short time later, outside the doctor's office, he stood suspended in the warm October sunshine—totally alone. It was Friday morning, October 13, 1995, the day his world, as he had always known it, ended. Cars sped by on the busy street. An old man was having an animated conversation with a young woman in overalls and a white tee shirt. The orange and red leaves of a nearby maple tree were still hanging on for dear life, knowing that they too would soon be swept away. He heard the sound of a bird as if it were coming from a faraway, distant land. The drive home felt like an out-of-body experience. He pulled into the driveway, only to come home to an empty house. Then he remembered that his wife, Sandy, had gone to a school function with their son. The empty house intensified the strange feelings that were rushing through his body. Hearing only the sounds of birds chirping and his own shoes thumping against the pavement, Tommy walked back out onto the street praying silently to the God he thought he knew but who now turned away from him. There were no words that could convey what he was feeling at that moment.

The rhythm of his shoes against the pavement was broken by the voice of a friend shouting, "Tommy! Tommy!" When he turned, he saw a man smiling at him over the top of a storm window. It was Adrian, a member of his congregation.

Tommy had begged God, "If you have turned from me, give me someone to be with me. I can't do this alone." He needed something to hang on to in the face of the approaching storm. Hearing his name called was as if he had heard God audibly speaking his name, calling him back to the present reality.

Adrian set his storm window on the ground next to the house where he was working and ran toward Tommy. Grinning, he grasped Tommy's hand. "How are things going, Tommy?" he asked in greeting.

Receiving the greeting as a question, Tommy responded, "Well, not too well right now. I just came back from my doctor's office, and I'm trying to process her words to me."

Tommy began to tell his story, and Adrian's words of comfort for Tommy were more than just the words of a caring friend; Tommy heard God saying that He would be with him every step of the way. While all the color had been drained out of his world, a world that was being ripped apart, he had to believe that God would not totally abandon him in the midst of the oncoming storm.

For Reflection

"But if you suffer for doing good and you endure it, this is commendable before God. To this you were called, because Christ suffered for you, leaving you an example, that you should follow in his steps" (I Peter 2:20*b*-21).

". . .Lord, to whom shall we go? You have the words of eternal life" (John 6:68).

All of us have experienced crises. Like Tommy, when crisis strikes, we also seek someone to turn to, someone to walk with us through the crisis. As you look back on the crises in your own life, to whom did you turn?

Did you find "Jesus with hands" in another?

How did God nevertheless meet you in the midst of your crisis?

Chapter 2
"Life Planner"

> *W*hen God gets us alone
> by affliction, heartbreak, or temptation,
> by disappointment, sickness...
> when He gets us absolutely alone,
> and we are dumbfounded,
> and cannot ask one question,
> then He begins to expound.

Oswald Chambers,
My Utmost for His Highest

He had been diagnosed in October. The brilliant hues of the leaves that had fallen to the ground in October faded, and the remaining crumpled fragments were swept away by the brisk November winds. It was now December.

Tommy leaned back and pushed his chair away from the desk. He turned to the window and gazed out at the one-hundred-year-old barren oak trees that stood on the hill alongside the church. This church, his dream, had been built on eighty acres of rolling hills. Its sprawling structure, three stories tall, situated in the middle of several new housing additions, would have been any pastor's dream; but this church had been *his* dream. He breathed deeply and reconnected to the moment, turning back to his computer and the task at hand, the Sunday sermon. Picking up where he left off...

Last Friday, I ventured toward Castleton Shopping Center to buy the 1996 date book for my handy *Franklin Planner*. I love even the thought of a new date book and all the extra stuff one can buy to put in it; all guaranteed to make one's life more efficient and organized. There is an incredible sense of hope that springs up within me as I neatly arrange those pages of blank squares into my official yearly planning notebook.

I may have told you before, in years past, how each of those blank squares becomes a symbol for me. Each square represents a part of my life for the coming year. One person, making this same observation, called each square an episode of his life. I like that. Looking forward to 1996, 366 episodes laid out, 366 episodes of life.

As I think back on the 344 episodes that I have already lived this year, I can see how I have filled them with office hours, church services, committee meetings, lunch meetings and various appointments. And these are only the things I couldn't afford to forget.

There have been a ton of things I do that never get written in my date book, such as mowing the lawn, taking a walk or eating supper. Only three months ago at a funeral service, I had used this mental picture of a yearly planner with its daily squares as a way for each of us to view our life. I had said, "None of us knows how many squares we have left." Even though no one knows about tomorrow, I asked those listening to me to imagine having 1,029 squares left in their life planner.

Looking back, I can't help but be amused by the irony of this message. Only one week later, a doctor gave me a surprisingly similar time frame for my life...

The diagnosis that had come in October was already beginning to manifest itself in the nuances of complex movements that Tommy had always taken for granted. The act of clicking his pen was only one of the many unconscious movements that he was now denied. Yes, Tommy was giving serious thought as to which square on his planner would be his last.

The whirlwind of Christmas activities that goes with pastoring a church had kept him focused on what was going on around him, and it wasn't until the beginning of February that an episode on Tommy's planner caught him totally by surprise. The whole thing unfolded like a Three Stooges movie.

Tommy, a high-energy person, was usually up by five in the morning, and even in the middle of January he would run a few miles out into the country. This day had begun like so many other days. He arrived at the office, prayed, read for a while, and began organizing what was to come that day by going through some notes and memos on his desk. For several weeks he had been experiencing severe pain in his arms, but he had attributed the pain to the ALS. On this particular morning there was a men's prayer breakfast in the church basement. Tommy took his pain medicine and went down to the men's breakfast. This time the pain became excruciating. He felt nauseated, weak, and short of breath. He attributed the queasiness and stabbing pain to indigestion. Nevertheless, Tommy excused himself and headed back up to his office. The next thing he knew, he was lying on the floor next to his computer with a church member standing over him. He soon learned that he had been lying there for over an hour. When he became flushed and clammy, he was carried outside. One parishioner called Tommy's neurologist and was told that what was going on had nothing to do with ALS. At that point, he was dragged back inside. There were people standing over him, phone calls, people staring at him, questions, police persons, police cars, EMTs, ambulances, and sirens; and all the while Tommy was sure that whatever was happening to him would soon go away. It wasn't until he was rushed to the hospital in an ambulance that he could admit that maybe what was happening to him might be more than just a mild case of indigestion. As the curtains of his denial began to lift, Tommy began to experience true pain.

With lightning speed two men wheeled him into the emergency room where a very young physician leaned over him and said, "Sir, you are in the middle of a major heart attack." It would have been enough for the young doctor to have said, "Sir, you are having a heart attack," but, no, he had said, "a major heart attack!"

Perhaps the great pain of letting go of life had literally flooded his heart with agony, creating an 85 percent blockage. But God was not going to allow the heart attack to be the last square on Tommy's planner. Tommy would have more squares in which to live, more episodes of letting go of all that he held near and dear, even life itself.

His do-it-yourself energy could no longer take action. In the days and months that followed, Tommy would consciously move square by square through his life planner, actively waiting on God as he watched his muscles atrophy one by one and his nervous system shut down. In all of his almost fifty years, he had never felt so vulnerable.

For Reflection

" . . . *The race is not to the swift or the battle to the strong, nor does food come to the wise or wealth to the brilliant or favor to the learned; but time and chance happen to them all. Moreover, no man knows when his hour will come* . . ." (Ecclesiastes 9:11b-12a).

" . . .*I will come like a thief, and you will not know at what time I will come to you*" (Revelation 3:3*b*).

Having been born into this time-space continuum, we have been given "an hour and a day." If God opened the book of life for you, and you could see how many squares you had left on your life planner, how would knowing change the way you lived today?

If you knew that you had only six months left to live, what would become the focus of your life?

If you knew that you would be called home in six days, what would be the first thing that you would want to do when you woke up tomorrow morning?

Chapter 3
"I Have Learned"

God engineers circumstances
and whatever they may be like
we have to see that we face them
while abiding continually with Him.

Oswald Chambers,
My Utmost for His Highest

Live and Learn and Pass it On[1]—he laid the book down next to the neat pile of notes left by Karen, his secretary. In one week Tommy would turn fifty. It had been less than four months since he had been diagnosed with ALS, but even in the early stages of this disease, he could feel the foreboding of the up-and-coming storm. Ever since the diagnosis, people asked about his game plan. He usually answered by explaining the medical options, the nutritional options, and some of the "alternative" avenues that he would be pursuing. He suspected that God did and could use all of these as "windows" through which He would pour His blessings. Having said all of that, he would go on to explain how his best energies were being given to putting himself in proper alignment to recognize God's will for his life in the midst of this incurable, progressive disease. That meant that he would spend his time praying, reading Scripture, being with those who encouraged his faith, and receiving the prayers and love of God's people—all the while trying to pass on what he had and was learning.

Still, it was difficult to look ahead. There were so many things that Tommy cherished—his wife, Sandy, and their three kids, Emily, Sarah, and Luke; the church that was so much a part of who he was and what he did; friends, family, and neighbors; and even the books that over the years had become his friends and mentors. Looking ahead to the next two or three years meant letting go of all he treasured, all those things that defined him and kept him focused in this life.

However, a book he had just read was challenging him. In this book the author had decided on the occasion of his fifty-first birthday to write, "I have learned that..." twenty times down the left side of a sheet of paper. The author then spent the rest of the day completing the sentences. The experience was so stimulating for him that he repeated it every Sunday morning. Then the thought hit him, "Why not begin collecting 'I have learned that...' statements from others?" The author's compilation of "I have learned that..." statements provoked Tommy's thinking.

The ones collected from children were especially poignant. One seven-year-old had written, "I've learned that you can't hide a piece of broccoli in a glass of milk."

Another said, "I've learned that if you spread the peas out on your plate, it looks like you ate more."

And still another said, "I've learned that my best friend is my teddy bear. He never tells my secrets."

The statements made by adults blended humor and insight. Like the one by the guy who said, "I've learned that even when I have pains, I don't have to be a pain." Tommy was trying hard to learn that lesson himself.

He laughed at the duffer who said, "I've learned that the quickest way to meet people is to pick up the wrong golf ball on the golf course."

Some of the more serious discoveries brought Tommy back to his present reality. "I've learned that you can do something in an instant that will give you a heartache for life." During his years of pastoring, he had seen people whose unconscious reactions and failed choices forever altered the course of their lives and the lives of those around them.

But the one that struck home was the one that said, "I've learned that the great challenge of life is to decide what's important and to disregard everything else." There were only so many squares left on his life planner. Tommy had half a century of memories, half a century of life lived and lessons learned.

He straightened up in his chair and with pen in hand, Tommy began to write, "I have learned that..."

He thought back to the small parsonage next to the church his father pastored in Evansville, Indiana. He had fond memories of those growing-up years. There had been grand adventures on the Ohio River (without his parents' permission). And he remembered constructing a huge maze of cardboard boxes on one of those seemingly endless sunny days of childhood.

It was in the front room of that parsonage, at six years of age, that Tommy learned one of the first lessons of his life. Tommy's dad was sitting in the old green lounge chair next to the picture window. He reached into the pocket of his suit pants and pulled out two shiny quarters. "Tommy, you are about to receive your first allowance," his father had said in his pulpit voice. Visions of financial independence glimmered in Tommy's head as his dad went on to explain the duties that went with earning this pricey sum. Tommy couldn't remember the list of responsibilities that came with his first earnings, but on that day his father taught him a lesson about money that impacted his whole life. With clear and measured words, his father continued, "Tommy, the tithe of your allowance is holy and belongs to the Lord."

At six years of age, Tommy didn't understand much about fractions or percentages; but this was a lesson learned that became a guiding principle for the rest of his life. As an adult, there had been times when his hand would shake and he would hesitate before writing the check. But even when larger sums of money were involved, the Lord would remind him of the lesson learned that day.

Tommy completed the first sentence on his piece of paper. "I have learned that…no matter how huge the tithe check, it is still only one nickel out of every fifty cents."

On the next line on his sheet of paper, Tommy scratched out "I have learned that…" and wrote "the most important thing that I have learned in life is…." He thought for a moment and then continued, "that if I get stuck on yesterday's failures or successes or worry about what might happen tomorrow, I will miss the here and now."

Others had learned the same thing. He remembered reading what the chaplain of the United States Senate had said: "I have to overcome my yesterdays, hold firm to a magnificent obsession for my tomorrows, and live today as if it were the only day I had left."

But for Tommy, it was Jesus who said it best. "But seek first his kingdom and his righteousness, and all these things will be given to you as well. Therefore do not worry about tomorrow, for tomorrow will worry about itself. Each day has enough trouble of its own" (Matthew 6:33-34).

He knew that the apostle Paul had learned the same life lesson. Picking up his Bible, he thumbed through the worn pages until he came to Philippians 3:13. "Brothers, I do not consider myself yet to have taken hold of it. But one thing I do: Forgetting what is behind and straining toward what is ahead, I press on toward the goal to win the prize for which God has called me heavenward in Christ Jesus." Tommy wanted Paul's words to become his words. He wanted to forget what was behind and live in the here and now without fearing what was to come.

Nevertheless, all the wisdom and lessons learned by these great minds did not ease his strain. This brutal, unforgiving enemy continued to suck the strength out of every muscle in his body. Short of a miracle, and he was prone to believe in miracles, Tommy was about to learn how to hold firm to the magnificent obsession of believing Christ for all his tomorrows and living today as if it were his last.

$\mathcal{F}$or $\mathcal{R}$eflection

"The ax is already at the root of the trees, and every tree that does not produce good fruit will be cut down and thrown into the fire" (Matthew 3:10).

We put our best energy into those things that are most meaningful to us. Is what you are putting your best energy into—i.e., your family, your job, your home, your future—producing good fruit?

"Let the wise listen and add to their learning, and let the discerning get guidance. . ." (Proverbs 1:5).

If you were to write, "I have learned . . ." twenty times down the left side of a sheet of paper, how would you complete those sentences?

Chapter 4
"The Potter's House"

God pays no respect to anything

we bring to Him.

There is only one thing God wants of us,

and that is our unconditional surrender.

Oswald Chambers,
My Utmost for His Highest

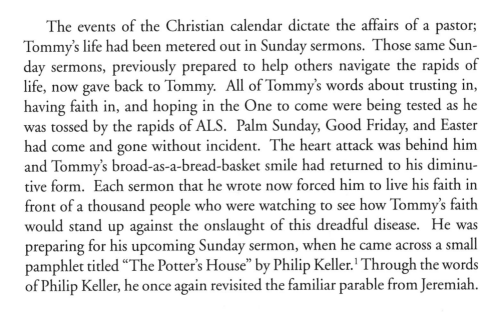

The events of the Christian calendar dictate the affairs of a pastor; Tommy's life had been metered out in Sunday sermons. Those same Sunday sermons, previously prepared to help others navigate the rapids of life, now gave back to Tommy. All of Tommy's words about trusting in, having faith in, and hoping in the One to come were being tested as he was tossed by the rapids of ALS. Palm Sunday, Good Friday, and Easter had come and gone without incident. The heart attack was behind him and Tommy's broad-as-a-bread-basket smile had returned to his diminutive form. Each sermon that he wrote now forced him to live his faith in front of a thousand people who were watching to see how Tommy's faith would stand up against the onslaught of this dreadful disease. He was preparing for his upcoming Sunday sermon, when he came across a small pamphlet titled "The Potter's House" by Philip Keller.[1] Through the words of Philip Keller, he once again revisited the familiar parable from Jeremiah.

> This is the word that came to Jeremiah from the Lord: "Go down to the potter's house, and there I will give you my message." So I went down to the potter's house, and I saw him working at the wheel. But the pot he was shaping from the clay was marred in his hands; so the potter formed it into another pot, shaping it as seemed best to him.
>
> Then the word of the Lord came to me: "O house of Israel, can I not do with you as this potter does?" declares the Lord. "Like clay in the hand of the potter, so are you in my hand, O house of Israel" (Jeremiah 18:1-6).

The image of the potter's house came alive as Tommy read from the pamphlet. He could imagine the remote mid-Eastern village where, with the passing of the centuries, little had changed. For generations too numerous to number, the local commerce and trade had continued to operate in the same manner, day after day, season after season, year after year. Tommy could see himself walking down a crowded street with vendors selling their handicrafts—carvings whittled from gnarled olive branches, colorfully woven shawls, brass and silver hammered bowls and utensils, and, of course, the beautifully shaped pieces of the village potter. He could feel the jostling of the crowds as he wound his way through the bustling narrow streets dotted with crude carts filled with fresh fish. He could smell the mingling scents of spices, perfumes, and the fish. He could hear the din of voices and the jingling of camel bells as he searched for the potter's shop. He could envision the aged potter with stooped shoulders and a deeply creased face. Tommy, placing himself in the story, entered the dim shop of the potter. Suddenly the potter looked up, squinting at the rush of sunlight through the now open door.

"Glad to have customers," he said to Tommy as Tommy examined an exquisite goblet, turning it around and around in his hands. On a stoop near the goblet sat a red clay pitcher. Tommy respectfully lifted the pitcher and rubbed his hand over its smooth surface. He made his way around the room taking time to hold each piece in turn, reflecting on its grace and beauty.

Tommy showed such interest that the potter invited him to watch while he worked the wheel. Tommy followed the potter as he slowly felt his way back through dark rooms until they came upon something resembling a lean-to attached to the back of the house. In the floor of the lean-to was a pit from which a vile and repulsive smell of decay leaped up at them. The old potter, ignoring the nauseating stench, kneeled beside the hole, and to Tommy's disbelief, plunged his fist into the pit, drawing up a dark mass of clay, and with his hands immediately began to mold it.

The old gentleman explained how he had learned his craft as a child from the great masters of another land known for its excellent pottery and how he had worked for many years as an apprentice to these, the greatest of potters.

Tommy's memory was drawn to his own apprenticeship. He was raised in the home of a Pentecostal preacher. Going to church was not a spectator sport. In the church of his apprenticeship, the congregation clapped their hands and said, "Amen," aloud whenever the occasion warranted it. Sometimes the Spirit would induce them to stand and sing songs with enthusiasm and vigor, camp meeting songs like "When the Roll is Called Up Yonder" and "I'll Fly Away." Tommy could remember singing "We're Marching to Zion" and picturing himself marching ever upward to glory; the song, thus, became a part of his personal story.

As he re-envisioned the visit to the potter's house, he was reminded of a song that he hadn't heard sung in almost twenty years, "He Brought Me Out of the Miry Clay." As a child, he had thought it was a strange song with strange words. Years later he learned that the words of that song came from the Fortieth Psalm. "I waited patiently for the Lord; / he turned to me and heard my cry. /He lifted me out of the slimy pit, /out of the mud and mire...." He remembered how he, too, had lived in darkness and how, when he was separated from his Creator in a pit as dark and slimy as his mind could imagine, the Master Potter had reached down and pulled him out. As Tommy watched the old potter molding the lump of clay with his fit, practiced hands, he could visualize God, the Master Potter, pressing him into a round, smooth ball, perfectly suited for His purposes. God was putting pressure on Tommy's life, transforming his character and shaping his soul.

A phrase from the next line of the Fortieth Psalm ran through Tommy's head: "he set my feet on a rock...." Tommy could imagine, in the center of the potter's house, a massive round slab of stone, a crudely cut rock that had been chiseled out from the side of a nearby mountain. Even in his wildest imagination, though, what Tommy could not fathom was how the old potter had moved the stone from the mountain to this his place of work. Here the potter would place his piece of clay and begin fashioning a vessel according to his purposes. God had lifted Tommy out of the slimy pit of his old self-life and placed him on a Solid Rock. And now, as Tommy imagined the old potter spinning the stone, he wondered if he could survive such a process—that of God spinning the stone and forming him into a vessel in accordance with God's own purposes.

Over the past five decades the Master Potter had already removed many pieces of grit from Tommy's life. Did the Master Potter's experienced fingers again find something in the clay that would mar the vessel he wanted to fashion? The will and the skill of The Master Potter were set on making something beautiful, but what about Tommy's will? Could he align his will with that of his Creator regardless of what that would mean for him in the days and months ahead? He did not know whether he was being shaped and molded into a noble goblet, fit to contain the fine wine of Christ's own life, or molded into a clay bowl into which others only dabbled their fingers. He knew what happened as Jeremiah watched the potter at his work. "But the pot he was shaping from the clay was marred in his hands; so the potter formed it into another pot, shaping it as seemed best to him" (Jeremiah 18:4).

There was certainly a Sunday sermon in the message from the potter's house, but what was becoming clearer to Tommy was that he must be willing to surrender all to God's forming work in his life. Whether he was being shaped into a noble goblet or a mere finger bowl did not matter; like the clay in the hand of the potter, so he must be in the hands of his Lord:

> Have Thine own way, Lord! Have Thine own way!
> Thou art the Potter, I am the clay. Mould me and make me
> After Thy will, While I am waiting, Yielded and still.[2]

For Reflection

✳ *"Consider it pure joy, my brothers, whenever you face trials of many kinds, because you know that the testing of your faith develops perseverance"* (James 1:2).

✳ *"Not only so, but we also rejoice in our sufferings, because we know that suffering produces perseverance (pressure); perseverance, character; and character, hope"* (Romans 5:3).

The Master Potter put pressure on Tommy's life, transforming his character and shaping his soul. How is God putting pressure on your life?

What is the difference between pressure that is from God and that which feels like pressure, but is an attack from Satan?

What is God calling you to surrender to him?

Chapter 5

"Of Monks and Fruitcakes"

*T*he great crisis is the surrender of the will.

When once the surrender has taken place…

We do not need to care what our circumstances are,

Jesus is amply sufficient.

Oswald Chambers,
My Utmost for His Highest

"What am I, a Protestant minister, doing here in a Catholic monastery surrounded by twenty thousand fruitcakes?" Tommy asked himself in disbelief as he looked around at his new home for the next three weeks. It was November, thirteen months since he had been diagnosed with ALS. He had questions, a myriad of questions. Tommy's symptoms had progressed as should have been expected in an ordinary man. Not that Tommy saw himself as a hero, far from it, but he was a man of God who had lived with the illusion that he was in control. For sixteen years he had delivered almost all of the Sunday morning sermons, performed all the weddings, and presided over all the funerals that took place in his church. As if that were not enough, Tommy prided himself in attending every open house and every graduation, and he still found time to speak on demand for almost any occasion. This had added up to over seventy hours per week, every week during his church career. He lived life packed to the max, without any spaces. He had tried to do it all, and when he was diagnosed with ALS, he had assumed that he could funnel this same do-it-yourself energy into controlling the symptoms of this disease.

However, by the end of the first year he knew that this storm was not going to pass over quickly. He had lost almost all of the strength in his hands and arms. This same weakness had now progressed to his legs. He had trouble speaking. Sometimes, like a drunk, although Tommy had never been a drinking man, he slurred his words. The muscles in his face were also affected, and it became increasingly difficult to form words. Living with so much loss and in this dark night of his soul, he had sought refuge in this sequestered monastery in Missouri. There were no phones to answer, no appointments to keep. In fact, he was so far from civilization that even a cell phone couldn't reach a cellular tower. There were no daily rituals to distract him. The only distraction in this outpost was the baking of fruitcakes for the Christmas season by the cloister of seventeen monks. A total of twenty thousand cakes were sent out to stores all over the world. He at least now knew that the rumor of there being only one fruitcake that was passed around year after year was not true. Apart from fruitcake to eat and jokes about fruitcakes, it was here that he had come to find a place free from distractions, to open the doors of his heart as a holy guest house and invite God to enter. For the past year he had struggled with shock, denial, and depression. Tommy felt like the victim in some science fiction horror movie. Without warning this disease, like some bizarre intruder, had moved in and taken up residence in the dark recesses of his brain. Night after night, it would attack and kill motor neurons—those large nerve cells in his brain that sent messages to his muscles. His hands were the first part of his body to be affected. It became increasingly difficult to hold a book, shake hands, or type a sermon. Each morning he would wake up with a foreboding. What was going to be affected next? He remembered a few weeks back to the time when, the day after he had played a game of tennis with his son Luke, he couldn't even hold the tennis racket.

It wasn't long before this bizarre intruder had attacked the neurons that sent messages to his legs and feet. He was a devout runner, and he had not missed running in the 500 mini-marathon race in downtown Indianapolis for the last seventeen years. In fact, he ran his last race in May of 1996, four months after the major heart attack, all the while wondering how soon he would need a wheelchair.

As this uninvited guest ravaged his motor neurons, he continued to lose functioning in his muscles. The throat, tongue, and facial muscles were weakened, and he began to have trouble speaking—a humiliating experience for a preacher. His chest muscles were affected, increasing his difficulty in expanding and contracting his lungs. While all of these functions one by one were being stolen from him, his cognitive processes remained unaffected. His mind was clear, active, and alert as he experienced life-giving energy being sucked from him, leaving him more fatigued with each new day.

Tommy wondered about the expectations of church members. Did they think that this trip was like the one of Moses going to the mountain and that he, like Moses, would come back with his face aglow? Did they think that he would, with the aura of an Old Testament prophet, appear at the podium on Sunday morning with stone tablets on which would be written God's plan for him and for the church? (Others had told him that his diminutive form and bald head fit their perception of an Old Testament prophet.) But Tommy had no illusions. This trip was not one of Moses, going to the mountain but rather, it was more like Jesus, going to Gethsemane. Alone with his empty heart, Tommy began to meditate on Jesus, praying to his Father in the garden. Jesus, the Incarnate Son of God, praying through his tears, praying through blood-like drops of sweat, asking his Father to answer his prayer. Jesus was asking, "Is there some other way? Have I really understood your plan? I want to avoid this cup. Would you let it pass from me?"

Tommy was asking those same questions, all the while remembering the Father's answer to his own Son. This disease was certainly his bitter cup. He had come to this place to be alone with God, in hopes that the God-Guest would invade his heart and bring a different response for him. He also knew that getting alone with God would require him to respond to the Lord's question for him. "Tommy, are you willing to give me everything: your family, your church, your vocation, even your life?"

He didn't have a clue as to how to surrender everything to the Lord. He had thought of surrender, of giving up control, as a lifelong journey down a path that would lead him ultimately to resurrection on the other side. Long ago, as a young man in his father's church, he thought that he had counted the cost of the journey. Oswald Chambers says that it is going to cost the natural in us everything, not something. With each new loss the path grew narrower and darker, and he knew that he could not weather the storm at the end without choosing to let go of everything that belonged on this side of life. It was time for him to take all the good gifts that came from God and lay them at the feet of Jesus, never to pick them up again. There was Sandy, his wife of almost thirty years. She had remained by his side through all the storms of his adult life. Luke, his son, was only ten years old. How does one let go of his only son? And there were the girls: Sarah, now a young adult, and Emily, newly married to Jeff. Tommy allowed himself to feel the love he had for his wife and for each of his children. His mother, his father, and his church family were next. And finally, even the illusion of control over his own life was brought to the cross and laid at the feet of Jesus.

This painful process of offering all to God continued day and night. Tommy allowed his imagination to carry him to the feet of Jesus, laying down and letting go of all that had been given to him to have and to hold in this life. Much of what he held dear had been taken for granted. He had assumed that those he loved and all that he valued would be there forever. He loved his family but had given much of his time to the church, believing that one day there would be time enough to do all those little tasks that are so much a part of committed relationships. At times he would cry out to God, "It's so unfair, Lord!" He felt vulnerable, alone, and for the first time in his life, totally out of control. However, in his heart of hearts he knew that no matter how difficult this process of letting go was, the eternal reward of being conformed into the likeness of his Savior far exceeded these temporal blessings.

During Tommy's stay at the monastery, in the midst of this season of letting go, a letter came from a member of his church. It was a poem that she had written for him that simply read:

I seek your face, dear Father God, your servant please remember.
   He whispered softly in my ear, "Absolute surrender."
Your promises are surely good, my Healer and my Mender.
   What does your promise rest upon? "Absolute surrender."
Oh Lord, my heart cries out to You. You are my Strong Defender.
   Then the Lord spoke to my heart, "Absolute surrender."
Humbled by His mighty hand among each dying ember,
   What more will you require of me? "Absolute surrender." [1]

Absolute surrender!

For Reflection

"But seek first his kingdom and his righteousness, and all these things will be given to you as well" (Matthew 6:33).

"Come to me, all you who are weary and burdened, and I will give you rest. Take my yoke upon you and learn from me, for I am gentle and humble in heart, and you will find rest for your souls. For my yoke is easy and my burden is light" (Matthew 11:28-30).

Tommy lived most of his life with the illusion that he was in control. What are those things that you do to create the illusion of control?

Are there areas of your life where you feel out of control: i.e. in your marriage, in your relationship with your kids, in your job, in your finances, in your ability to change personal habits that are not good for you?

How would your life change if you took all those things that you held near and dear and laid them at the foot of the cross?

Chapter 6
"Am I Alone?"

*J*esus can expound nothing
until we get through
all the noisy questions of the head
and are alone with Him.

Oswald Chambers,
My Utmost for His Highest

"Real loneliness comes when we have lost all sense of having things in common," says Henri Nouwen in *The Return of the Prodigal Son.*[1] Of course, he was speaking of the loneliness of the prodigal son who, waking up in a foreign land, realized he had no money left to spend and no gifts left to give, that he was a person to whom no one showed any sign of recognition. Tommy, too, realized how much he relied on recognition and acceptance to feel connected to others. As a pastor he understood how communities, especially church communities, are created out of common backgrounds, histories, and religious beliefs. Common life-styles, customs, and language bind them together. He was acutely aware that everything that had given him a sense of belonging to someone or something larger than himself was slipping away. He felt disconnected.

Tommy was not lost in a foreign land feeding pigs; he was lost in a disease that was eating him alive. Some who knew he was sick believed God would heal him. That was the end of the matter. Still others, when they were with him, to some degree felt his pain but then went home to their families, friends, and jobs and allowed the considerations in their own worlds to carry them far from the day-to-day suffering that Tommy was experiencing. He was alone with his disease, swirling around in a torment of isolation that no one else could enter into. Searching for someone who could understand his isolation, someone else who had walked down this narrow, twisting path, Tommy turned to the Psalms for comfort.

God, God…my God!
 Why did you dump me

miles from nowhere?
Doubled up with pain, I call to God
    all the day long. No answer. Nothing.
I keep at it all night, tossing and turning.

Night after night Tommy tossed and turned, calling out to God. In his isolation, he screamed out:

And you! Are you indifferent, above it all,
    leaning back on the cushions of Israel's praise?
We know you were there for our parents:
    they cried for your help and you gave it;
    they trusted and lived a good life.

His parents, had they not built a large and prosperous church on faith? Had God not answered their prayers?

And here I am, a nothing—an earthworm,
    something to step on, to squash.
Everyone pokes fun at me;
    they make faces at me, they shake their heads:
"Let's see how God handles this one;
    Since God likes him so much, let *him* help him!"

After all, he was a pastor. Everyone was looking to see how God would handle him. Would he be healed? Would he pass into oblivion with no remembrance of who he was or what he had done, or did God purpose something yet unknown for him?

And to think you were midwife at my birth,
    setting me at my mother's breasts!
When I left the womb you cradled me;
    since the moment of birth you've been my God.
Then you moved far away

and trouble moved in next-door.
I need a neighbor.

Trouble had moved in next door—it was ALS. Tommy needed another neighbor, a friend, a confidant. Tommy needed someone to lead him through the approaching storm.

I'm a bucket kicked over and spilled,
    every joint in my body has been pulled apart.
My heart is a blob
    of melting wax in my gut.
I'm dry as a bone,
    my tongue black and swollen.
They have laid me out for burial
    in the dirt.
    (from Psalm 22, The Message)

If there were words to describe the torment of this disease, they would be found in the Psalms. It was here that Tommy could find a neighbor, a friend, a confidant—someone who understood his feelings. He was not totally alone; the psalmist had gone before him. Here was a sojourner whose wretchedness matched his. Tommy had found another whose words echoed his own despair. Like the psalmist, he too knew what it meant to have his heart "a blob of melting wax" and to be "dry as a bone." In fact, the psalmist with "a tongue black and swollen" even understood his struggle to force the muscles of his own tongue and mouth to form words. There was no way around the pain that he was experiencing, but at least he knew that others had traveled this path before him and found God to be faithful in the midst of what was and what was to come.

For Reflection

"How long, O Lord? Will you forget me forever? /How long will you hide your face from me? /How long must I wrestle with my thoughts /and every day have sorrow in my heart?" (Psalm 13:1-2a).

"If only my anguish could be weighed and all my misery be placed on the scales! It would surely outweigh the sand of the seas. . ." (Job 6:2-3a).

Most of us, in the midst of crisis, have felt totally alone in our pain. We believe that no one can understand how much we hurt, and we forget that God is with us. Can you remember a time in your life when you turned a corner only to find a twisting, dark path looming before you?

How did God meet you in that darkness?

Did a Psalm or another word from Scripture give you solace in your time of need?

Part 2

My life is like a faded leaf,
My harvest dwindled to a husk;
Truly my life is void and brief
And tedious in the barren dusk;
My life is like a frozen thing,
No bud nor greenness can I see:
Yet rise it shall—the sap of Spring;
O Jesus, rise in me.

— — — — — — — —

My life is like a broken bowl,
A broken bowl that cannot hold
One drop of water for my soul
Or cordial in the searching cold;
Cast in the fire the perished thing;
Melt and remould it, till it be
A royal cup for Him my King:
O Jesus, drink of me.

Christina Rossetti
"A Better Resurrection"

Chapter 7
"A Book is Born"

The author who benefits you most

is not the one who tells you

something you did not know before,

but the one who gives expression to the truth

that has been dumbly struggling in you for utterance.

Oswald Chambers,
My Utmost for His Highest

My stomach growled as I walked down the stairs after my last session before lunch. A church counselor, I had been at Northview Christian Life Church for almost thirteen years. During that time, many hours were spent with grieving people who were struggling with hard questions. For the past year many of those questions focused on Tommy's illness:

"If God is a good God, how can He allow this to happen to Tommy?"

"If God heals, why hasn't He healed Tommy?"

All the questions pertaining to Tommy's suffering revolved around one ultimate question: "If God allows this to happen to Tommy, how can I believe that He won't allow something similar to happen to me?"

We all want to believe in a good God. We all want to believe in a just God. And yet, when confronted with pain that appears meaningless and suffering that is unjust, we come face to face with our own core fear: "Can I trust a God who allows suffering and injustice to love me personally?"

In my own spiritual journey, I have befriended the questions and embraced the fear as being part of the mystery of God. My experience with those who had brought these questions to the counseling process confirmed to me that many in this congregation, some for the first time, were being confronted with a suffering that they could not rationalize, minimize, nor deny. Tommy Paino was visibly sick, sometimes depressed, and occasionally fearful.

I prayed, asking God if there was anything I could offer to help Tommy or the congregation process the changes that lay ahead. After much prayer, I felt a nudging to approach Tommy. When I arrived downstairs,

Tommy was sitting near the door to his office. It was time to act.

"Tommy, do you have a few minutes?" I asked, somewhat sheepishly, knowing that Tommy had already been inundated with letters, phone calls, and literature from faithful, well-meaning friends and acquaintances who thought that they knew what God's will was for him.

Sinking into the blue patterned couch near the bookcases in Tommy's office, I began, "Tommy, I'm never sure whether I am hearing from God or not, and I wouldn't presume to know what God intends for your future, but have you considered writing about what you are going through?"

This was not a new idea for Tommy. He too had entertained the possibility of writing a book. We talked about the effects of ALS on him personally and how having a pastor with a terminal illness impacted the church. After about forty-five minutes, we parted with an agreement that we would pray about this and enlist a group from the congregation to help us explore the possibility of a book.

Over the next few weeks, we put together what we called a focus group. Ten of us crowded into Tommy's office for the first meeting. Each person came with a different perspective, but one thing that we all had in common was that every one of us loved and respected Tommy, and every one of us was already grieving loss. Some were still in shock and disbelief. Others, whether out of denial or in faith, believed that God would miraculously heal Tommy. Still others had come to learn how they could be a part of helping the church community heal.

Even though Tommy was reluctant to be the center of attention at this first meeting, he nevertheless set the tone for what was to come. Tommy didn't want to be known as the pastor with a terminal illness, and he didn't want to tell a story about how he learned to cope with ALS—others had already done that.

"I think the story I would like to tell is how a church, a community of people, walk through a challenging time in the life of that community and what we as that community discover about ourselves," Tommy said to the group. "It seems that churches, as well as other organizations, rarely come into the kind of community that God intended. I have a strong sense that such a community would be magnetic and verify the power of the Gospel. My desire is that the kind of love and concern that has come my way would become the norm of this community." Tommy was speaking about the thousands of cards and letters that had already been delivered to his house and the myriad of little kindnesses that different people from within the community were already doing for him and his family, not to mention the untold number of prayers from around the world that had been offered up for his healing. However, it was what he said next that left me with a profound sense of what Tommy wanted to see happen through the writing of this book.

Looking around the room at the familiar faces of those Tommy knew and loved, he began, "Most of you know Jerry. Jerry is a man who is in the front row of this church every Sunday morning and worships God from his wheelchair. If I was Jerry, and I saw God heal Pastor Tommy, I would be so angry with God that He was such a respecter of persons. Jerry has lived his life in that wheelchair and God has not seen fit to heal him. It would seem unjust for God to heal me and leave so many others like Jerry in their suffering."

Tommy's words left the group struggling with the tension between God's providential will and His promise of healing.

"I wonder what would happen if we as a church chose to show the kind of forgiveness, the kind of acceptance, and the kind of love that you have shown me, but to those around us for whom we do not have such an affinity?" Tommy asked. "What if we almost tripped over each other doing for others the same things that you have done for me? Maybe, in some sense, we would come to know what it means to be family in the kingdom of God. We would change the world."

These were hard questions for all of us. Tommy was visible and loved by the church. It was easy to respond to his need. There were others who were less visible, less attractive, and less appreciative. Could a body of believers choose to love the unlovely, the irreverent, and those who could not reciprocate in kind with such a selfless love? That was the question Tommy posed to us that evening.

I thought about the story in Luke of the woman who had been subject to bleeding for twelve years. In chapter eight, Luke tells the story.

Now when Jesus returned, a crowd welcomed him, for they were all expecting him. Then a man named Jairus, a ruler of the synagogue, came and fell at Jesus' feet, pleading with him to come to his house because his only daughter, a girl of about twelve, was dying.

As Jesus was on his way, the crowds almost crushed him. And a woman was there who had been subject to bleeding for twelve years, but no one could heal her. She came up behind him and touched the edge of his cloak, and immediately her bleeding stopped.

"Who touched me?" Jesus asked.

When they all denied it, Peter said, "Master, the people are crowding and pressing against you."

But Jesus said, "Someone touched me; I know that power has gone out from me."

Then the woman, seeing that she could not go unnoticed, came trembling and fell at his feet. In the presence of all the people, she told why she had touched him and how she had been instantly healed. Then he said to her, "Daughter, your faith has healed you. Go in peace" (Luke 8:40-48).

As I read this story, I see a woman who is invisible—lost in the crowd like so many believers who are lost in the church because of their physical, emotional, and spiritual woundedness. According to the law, this woman was unclean. It would have been a grievous sin for her to touch a rabbi. Yet Jesus, on His way to the house of a ruler of the synagogue, a religious leader who was most likely highly respected, stopped to communicate with this woman of faith, a woman who had been a nonperson in the midst of the crowd. He didn't stop to condemn her for touching Him—I'm sure that is what the crowd, even the disciples, expected Him to do. Rather, He called her "Daughter," placing her healing in the context of relationship with Him.

If we could respond to those who are wounded and less visible in the way we have responded to Tommy, in the way Jesus responded to the woman who had been subject to bleeding for twelve years, we could indeed change the world.

For Reflection

"This is my command: Love each other" (John 15:17).

"If you love those who love you, what reward will you get? Are not even the tax collectors doing that? And if you greet only your brothers, what are you doing more than others?" (Matthew 5:46-47).

Tommy talked about the type of community that a church would have to become to respond to others as God intended. He had received an outpouring of unconditional love and acceptance from those in the church who knew and loved him. His question to each of us is "how do we, as part of a community of believers, personally respond to 'the least of these' with unconditional love and acceptance?"

Do you believe that it is possible to respond to those with whom we have little affinity in the same way that we respond to those we know and love?

If you believe that loving others in that way could change the world, what stops you from reaching out to those who are most in need of that kind of love?

Chapter 8
"The Remembering One"

*T*he circumstances of a saint's life

are ordained of God.

In the life of a saint

there is no such thing as chance.

Oswald Chambers,
My Utmost for His Highest

Tommy was a neatnik. Everything in his office spoke to this fact. The polished top of his mahogany desk only displayed those pieces of paper and writing instruments that were absolutely needed to perform his daily tasks as a pastor. The shelves of books in Tommy's study were alphabetized by the author's last name. Many of the saints and sages that were present on those shelves became a part of our conversations—St. John of the Cross, Thomas Aquinas, Oswald Chambers, C. S. Lewis, Calvin Miller, Philip Yancey, and Paul Tillich—just to name a few. There were also shelves of Bibles in his study—the Berkeley Bible, the King James Bible, the New English Bible, the Amplified Bible, the Good News Bible, The Message, and on and on—translations, interpretations, paraphrases, and commentaries, all tutors of the Good News. These books and Bibles were a part of Tommy's story. They, along with his family, shaped Tommy's view of God, himself, and others. All, at one time or another, were companions with him on his spiritual journey.

"Tommy, before we begin this project, would you tell me about your family of origin and how they have influenced you spiritually?" I asked in my most receptive counseling voice.

Tommy, moving into a thinking mode, rolled his eyes up as he began. "All of us have a story to live. Finding that story and living it out is part of the fun of being human. Telling the story anchors our faith. When we quit telling our stories, or no longer have people who believe them, we lose our way.

"While reading *The Silence of Adam*, I came across something that I had never read before. Genesis 1:27 reads, 'So God created man in his own image, in the image of God he created him; male and female he created them.' Larry Crabb, in *The Silence of Adam*, states that the word 'man,' translated from the Hebrew word, *zakar*, means 'the remembering one.' Man is the one who remembers. In the relationship of male and female, the male is uniquely responsible for remembering what God has done in the past and speaking it into the present.[1] Since reading that, I have brought to remembrance my heritage. I have never been intrigued by my physical genealogy, but I am intrigued by my spiritual genealogy.

"My grandfather, as a young man, emigrated to the United States from Italy," Tommy continued. "He was from a staunch Catholic family. His first wife contracted tuberculosis, and at that time there was no known cure. My grandfather heard of an evangelist, Mrs. M. B. Woodworth-Etter, who resided in Indianapolis, Indiana. He left his home in Tupper Lake, New York, and traveled to Indianapolis to seek healing prayer for his wife.

"Even though my grandfather's first wife died from the tuberculosis, Maria Woodworth-Etter so influenced my grandfather that he eventually left Tupper Lake for good, returning to Indianapolis to became a part of her ministry. My grandfather recalled that after praying for eight weeks, on December 26, 1919, he received the baptism of the Holy Spirit. It was a time of tent revivals and Pentecostal manifestations, miracles, signs, and wonders. All that he had seen and experienced convinced him of the reality of this personal God in Jesus Christ.

"It was in the Woodworth-Etter Tabernacle on the west side of Indianapolis that my grandfather met my grandmother. Immediately after he and my grandmother were married (she was only sixteen years old at the time), they launched into full-time ministry with M. B. Woodworth-Etter. Thousands came to know Jesus Christ through that ministry, and many were healed or delivered with powerful signs and wonders following. Maria Woodworth-Etter was a powerful evangelist. As many as twenty thousand people would show up to hear her speak. Night after night, great numbers of people became a part of that movement of God. Maria Woodworth-Etter's ministry predated the 1900's Azusa Street Revival. It was right after the Civil War, when she was only sixteen years of age, that she heard the call of God and began preaching. She preached throughout Ohio, Illinois, Indiana, Kentucky, and Missouri and gained a following of thousands.

"It was a time of Pentecostal revival and my grandfather was on the cutting edge of this sweeping movement. He and my grandmother traveled throughout the Midwest preaching in tents with Maria Woodworth-Etter. After each revival, my grandfather and grandmother would stay and establish a storefront ministry in that community before moving on. My dad was raised under this full-blown, old-time Pentecostal ministry. That is the heritage of Lakeview Temple, my father's church. Both my spiritual heritage and my father's spiritual heritage are directly connected to this old lady's ministry.

"After Maria Woodworth-Etter passed away, my grandfather was invited to pastor the Woodworth-Etter Tabernacle. My grandfather eventually handed the mantle to my father, who established Lakeview Temple in that place on the west side of Indianapolis. I grew up in that church with its theology deeply rooted in the sweeping Pentecostal movement of the early 1900s. As a kid, I remember the crutches and wheelchairs that hung on the walls in testimony to the healings and miracles that had taken place there. I am sure that all of that has deeply affected the formation of my own theology."

"Tommy, as a child growing up in that movement, what were those messages that informed your understanding of God in Christ?" I asked as I fumbled to turn over the tape in the tape player.

"Every sermon was a combination of four things. The sermons that I heard during the first twenty-one years of my life were always variations on those four themes: 'All sinners need to be saved.' 'Christ can come at any moment—be ready or be left behind.' 'In the last days, God will pour out his Spirit on all flesh, and speaking in tongues is the proof of that,' and 'Jesus Christ came to heal the sick.'

"Our church was blue-collar through and through. These were people who packed their lunch pails day after day and went off to work in the factories. The world held little attraction for them, and the church was their only hope of escape from the drudgery and pain of their everyday hardworking existence. It wasn't until my generation that all that changed.

"My childhood was lived 'knowing' that Christ would return before I became a teenager. I 'knew' it. Now, it is hard to describe how a whole church of people could live that way. Holiness was paramount. We were not to do anything that could be considered less than pure. Every service ended with all of us at the altar. The problem was that we thought holiness could be obtained in outward forms: holy attire, holy talk, no movies, no skating, no dancing, mixed bathing, or card playing. I will never forget the time that my dad came home and found that I had bought a deck of cards. He went through the roof! Looking back, what we thought to be the pinnacle of spirituality was really the elementary, foundational stage. The emphasis on being holy and separate as a people became a schizophrenic split in that we never figured out how to be separate in such a way that holiness was attractive to others. We were either regarded as weird or elitist. Following the path of holiness can only happen through an act of grace.

"Having said all of this, I am intrigued by how difficult it is to develop spirituality in community. Everyone needs to go through all the stages of growth. Unfortunately, the church lacks *mentors*. Without mentors we get stuck in whatever stage the leadership rises to. It leaves us susceptible to every new wave that comes on the scene.

"One Sunday, when I was a young man, I drove my grandfather to Fort Wayne, Indiana. He was in his eighties then. I was hoping that during that drive he would reminisce about all that he had learned in his many years as a minister of the Gospel. I wanted to draw on the wisdom of his years. I remember the overwhelming disappointment that I felt when I realized he was still living out of what God had done in the past. His understanding of God in Christ had never moved beyond that foundational stage of spirituality.

"Even though the early church was in crisis mode, the apostle Paul somehow rose above all of that. I doubt if the church ever did. I think we are entering into a period of the development of the church where people are willing to leave the 'old tents' that are no longer relevant to this generation and move on as the cloud of God moves on. I wonder where this generation of the church will end up.

"My father, Thomas Paino, Jr., was the prototypical second generation of what was then a fresh movement of God's Spirit. Those who were willing to flow in the energy of that movement and give structure to it were the ones who built the Bible schools. What was taught in those schools emanated from a first generation memory of that movement.

"I am the prototypical third generation who has only a faint memory of what God did during that period of spiritual history. I am still trying to make sense of it all, looking at those basic elements and redefining them for this generation.

"Some years ago I went to hear Richard Foster speak at Marian College in Indianapolis. He is the author of *Celebration of Discipline* and *Freedom of Simplicity.*" Tommy glanced towards the shelves of books on the far side of the room. Tripping on the hem of my dress as I got up, I walked over to the books and pulled Richard Foster's books from the shelf as Tommy continued. "He describes the development of the different Christian movements as streams of Christianity. Every denomination flows from one of these streams or a combination of them.

"The first stream is composed of those who emphasize evangelism and taking the Gospel into all the world. Campus Crusade is an example of the kind of spiritual institution that is formed in that stream of Christianity. Their ministry testifies to the power of Christ carried forth by those who minister out of that stream. A man whose whole ministry flows from that stream is Billy Graham. His message of salvation has reached thousands, maybe even millions of people. That is evangelism at its best. The risk is that even though the Gospel message of salvation through belief in the resurrected Christ is a primary doctrine of the church, we can become so busy evangelizing that all other aspects of our Christian development are sacrificed. When we only view others through the lens of "saved" or "unsaved," we lose sight of the essence of salvation, which is to love others as the Father loves us.

"The second stream of Christianity spotlights holiness and living the virtuous life. At its best, it holds up a standard of behavior, deeply ingrained habits of virtue, that counters the erosion of morality in our contemporary society. Part of my training came from this holiness tradition. The danger is to become too caught up in our own sense of being holy and miss the One who is holy. We must become a holy people without becoming 'holier-than-thou.'

"A third stream of Christianity is the Incarnational or Sacramental stream. We have given the rights to the sacraments and the symbolic to the high church: the Catholics and the Episcopalians. The sacraments, the bread and the wine, have kept Christ alive for two thousand years. The tendency is to continue the ritual of communion and forget Who it is that the communion celebrates.

"The fourth stream, one that is almost lost to this generation and this culture, is the Contemplative stream. It has to do with the prayer-filled life and fanning the flames of our 'First Love,' Jesus Christ. The desert fathers and mothers, Saint John-of-the-Cross, Teresa of Avila, and others who have lived cloistered lives are examples of this stream. If our personal revelation and communion with God excludes going into all the world and building community with our fellow sojourners, then we cease to be of any earthly good. Without purifying our motives, we always have a tendency to get out of balance.

"Another stream of Christianity is the Social Justice stream. It is about living the compassionate life with all people. Jesus exemplified this when he said, 'The Spirit of the Lord is upon me, because he has anointed me to bring good news to the poor' (Luke 4:18). It is easy for us to become so comfortable that we don't want to look beyond our paved driveways and manicured lawns and 'bring good news to the poor.'

"The Charismatic-Pentecostal movement makes up the sixth stream of Christianity. It emphasizes the manifestation of the gifts of the Holy Spirit. My spiritual heritage also flows from the waters of that stream of Christianity. If all we do as Christians is to emphasize the gifts and work-ing of the Holy Spirit, we err in the development of our faith, that day-by-day walking out 'the substance of things hoped for, but not seen.' We seem to get bogged down in seeking the gifts of God rather than God, the Giver of all gifts.

"A mature spirituality is formed in the river where all six streams run together.[2] That is why, if I weren't a pastor, I don't know where I would go to church. It would be difficult for me to find a church that reflects where I am today. A church takes a giant step when it acknowledges all six streams as a part of spiritual development. By temperament and pref-erence, most of us are drawn towards one stream or another. It is a balancing act to hold all six streams in tension.

"There have been moments of inspiration when I know that I have entered the flow of one of the other streams of Christianity. The breaking out of the Charismatic-Pentecostal stream came when I entered Christian Theological Seminary in the early seventies. It decimated all of my neat categories without giving me anything in return. I felt like a swarm of locusts had devoured my spiritual landscape and left it desolate. What emerged from that experience was the ability to see other streams of Christianity. I left Christian Theological Seminary and went to Fuller. Fuller was a safe haven where, after having my fundamental beliefs dismantled, I could begin to reconstruct what I knew to be true. It was an environment of faith. I was free to ask the hard questions, wrestle with the same issues as before, but in a community of people who had walked the same path and were not threatened by my questions. They supported and helped me as I shaped my own reality.

"Fuller at that time was Evangelical in the best sense of the word. Fuller was embroiled in the controversy over 'the battle for the Bible.' It was walking a tightrope between neo-Evangelism and Fundamentalism. Fuller as an institution embraced the belief that the Bible is the inspired Word of God, but it recoiled from the belief that the Bible is inerrant, that it is without error.

"At the same time that all of this was going on, there was a professor at Fuller who was teaching a class on 'Signs and Wonders,' exposing both the student body and the faculty to healing, miracles, and speaking in tongues. Here in this environment was a strange mix of Fundamentalism, Evangelicalism and Charismatic-Pentecostalism. In the midst of these merging streams was a group of professors and students who had a rich understanding of God's Word as inspired, relevant, and authoritative and were passionate about their faith and love of the Lord.

"This is kind of an aside story, but it illustrates the nature of that environment during that time. A Professor Barker taught the first class that I took. He was the academic dean. He taught this required course on the emergence of the church. This particular lecture was on the charismatic nature of the early church. Professor Barker brought in a tape, with the sounds of people speaking in tongues on it, to play for the class. He was about to push the 'play' button, but stopped to ask if anyone in the class had ever spoken in tongues. About eighty percent of the class raised their hand. I remember that it about knocked this guy's socks off. He said, 'Well, we don't need to play this tape, then.'

"What I learned in my seminary days at Fuller was that there was hope for the church and there was hope for me. That was a turning point in my spiritual journey. I could embrace my roots and at the same time not be afraid to enlarge my sense of who God is and what He is doing in the church in this day. I had spread my umbrella to include the Holiness tradition, Evangelicalism, and Charismatic-Pentecostalism. The Contemplative, the Social Justice tradition, and the Sacramental came later for me in different ways.

"I have always been intrigued by the lives of those men and women who have chosen a contemplative way of knowing God. I have read many of the contemplative writers. The earliest contemplatives go back to the desert fathers and mothers, those men and women who, within a few hundred years after the birth of Christ, left the cities and traveled to the deserts of northern Africa, thirsting for a deeper understanding of God. Many of them for years lived in destitution on the edge of the desert, separated from others in order to live a life of prayer and contemplation. Over the years I have had a few isolated encounters with those who have chosen this way. Gradually my own journey has run parallel to and eventually merged into the Contemplative stream of Christianity.

"The sense of the Sacramental came to me through an unusual set of circumstances. About seven years ago, I went on what the Episcopalians call a Cursillo Walk. I was one of only two non-Episcopalians on that walk. My interest in that retreat weekend was to find a prototype for retreats for the Northview community. It was there that I began to rediscover the sacramental."

I looked down at my watch with amazement. It was two o'clock. I was supposed to be upstairs in a counseling session at that very moment. "Tommy, I'm sorry. I haven't been paying attention to the time. I have to go." I gathered my papers and tape player and ran out the door, all the while wondering about the unusual circumstances Tommy was alluding to regarding the Cursillo Walk retreat weekend. Each interview with Tommy left me with unanswered questions. Was I getting in over my head, believing that I could pull all the pieces together in some coherent form and write this story? Already I had gathered hundreds of pages of notes. I wasn't sure whether I could muster enough confidence to follow through with the writing of this book. I stuck the thought on a shelf in my mind, along with the mental note to read something by Richard Foster, and shifted gears. It was time to focus on the needs of the young lady sitting in my office.

For Reflection

"This mystery is that through the gospel the Gentiles are heirs together with Israel, members together of one body, and sharers together in the promise in Christ Jesus" (Ephesians 3:6).

"The body is a unit, though it is made up of many parts; and though all its parts are many, they form one body. So it is with Christ"
(I Corinthians 12:12).

Our way of experiencing Christ is informed by our Christian heritage or lack thereof. Using Richard J. Foster's streams of Christianity, what streams of Christianity have you embraced?

Is there any one stream of Christianity that has significantly influenced your way of living the Christ-life?

What aspects of your Christian faith do you want to pass on to your children or others?

Chapter 9
"Undaunted Courage"

✳ *T*here is a continual testing in the life of faith,

and the last great test is death. . . .

Faith is unutterable trust in God,

trust which never dreams that He will not stand by us.

Oswald Chambers,
My Utmost for His Highest

"A couple of years ago I read *Undaunted Courage* by Stephen Ambrose[1]," Tommy said as I set my coffee mug on a magazine on his desk and quickly rummaged through my purse for a pen. At first I had taped all of our interviews, but now I could write as fast as Tommy could talk, providing I had a pen.

"It's the story of the Lewis and Clark expedition," he continued. " In 1803, President Thomas Jefferson commissioned Meriwether Lewis to make a journey across the northern continent in search of the fabled Northwest Passage. President Jefferson hoped that a passage would be found whereby it would be possible to navigate from the Atlantic Ocean to the Pacific Ocean. Meriwether Lewis traveled overland to Philadelphia. There he stopped to prepare himself, gathering men and supplies for the journey ahead. He advanced farther overland to the Ohio River, and from there traveled downstream to the Mississippi River. Reaching the juncture of the Ohio and Mississippi Rivers, Lewis and his band of men turned right, voyaging upriver to what is now the city of St. Louis. Again he gathered supplies and men for the journey west. After several more months of preparation, he and his band traveled up the Mississippi to its convergence with the Missouri River. The trail forged from that point on was through territory never before seen by white men. At long last they reached an Indian village in North Dakota, where they waited out a bitter winter.

"With the coming of spring, Lewis's band took to the river again. They expected to voyage downriver all the way to the Continental Divide. From there, they would portage, maybe half a day's journey, to the Columbia River and then gently float downstream to the Pacific Ocean.

"That was their intention. That was their full expectation. Nevertheless, as they reached the source of the Missouri River, and as they crested a rise in the plains that was indeed the foothills of the Continental Divide, they faced an insurmountable barrier. They had come up against the Rocky Mountains. It was late autumn and winter was biting at their heels. There was no turning back. Going forward meant entering the mountains, facing the terror of the unknown. I think about the shock and despair they must have experienced. Their whole journey is a parable for my life. I am in the Rocky Mountains, but I am still not convinced that I will come out on the other side. Here's my struggle: I'm already in the mountains, and there's no option of turning back. Do I dare believe that I will get through these mountains alive, and more importantly, does believing that I will get through alive help or hinder the journey?"

✳ I knew that Tommy, like Meriwether Lewis, had also been commissioned, but by One whose authority was greater than that of any president. He was commissioned for a spiritual journey. Early in his journey, Tommy traveled downstream, making good progress, moving gently forward with great anticipation. He had been commissioned to be a pastor. With eager expectation, he entered seminary and began to prepare himself for the journey ahead.

But after a while he, too, came to a juncture where two converging rivers met, and the waters began to flow against him. I am sure that Tommy experienced himself in this place on many occasions, but one incident was particularly memorable. Once during our talks, almost in passing, he said, "Do not sell your soul to anything that requires undue maintenance. In building this church, I found myself obligated to strange bedfellows and came close to losing my soul in the process. What I know is that God is building a people who are sojourners by nature, not a people who will chisel out a solid temple. I allowed the voices of others to become my conscience instead of the voice of God. Outside of a clear direction from God, one that gives you a deep peace—back off." Two rivers converged for Tommy, one of seeking God as the source of all things and one of seeking others for the resources to do all things. He had traveled upriver emotionally and spiritually to build this new church building. What he had not foreseen was that as he crested the rise of erecting a magnificent building, the Rocky Mountains of ALS, a life-taking disease, were on the other side. He would have liked to have romanticized this terror of ALS as being only symbolic, a place of transformation. God could heal him and from there he would float gently downstream to his destination—uninterrupted intimacy with his Heavenly Father. But Tommy knew that his own journey was patterned after Jesus' journey. Jesus, who had been commissioned by his Father, traveled a path that led to Golgotha and ultimately the cross. In the Garden of Gethsemane, Jesus crossed over his foothills and faced the mountains of his own destiny, the terror of the cross. If God did not spare his only Son, Tommy knew that he, too, might not come out on the other side.

"Tommy, how can daring to believe that you will get through these mountains hinder the journey?" I asked.

"In one of Robert Schuller's books there is a profile of a man who endured grave adversity and triumphed. He lived seventeen years on a breathing machine. Robert Schuller asked him if he had ever prayed to be healed.

"The man answered, 'Of course. But God finally healed me of my need to be healed.'

"Part of me says, 'Wow, what a breakthrough.' Another part of me says, 'Not so fast!' Are there only two options—one of anxiously striving to be healed and the other of having no need to be healed? Is it possible to be so detached from the flesh that being healed really doesn't matter? Is the true goal of life the giving up of all that matters? If it is, then we should pursue that at all cost. If that were the case, we could achieve that end by lopping off everything dear to us, eliminating all risks, and setting up camp in the mountains, waiting for the inevitable. But it has to be more than that. The 'more' has to be the will of the Father. I want to retreat to more substantial ground where there are answers, but that is not an option. I have to redeem my resolve to go on."

"Resolve to go on into what?" I asked, wondering what Tommy foresaw his future to be.

"I'm in a cloud of unknowing," Tommy responded. "T. S. Eliot said, 'We know we have arrived.' I want to see God partnering in this with me and then I will know I have arrived—whatever that may look like."

Tommy was referring to lines from "Little Gidding" in *Four Quartets* by T. S. Eliot.

> We shall not cease from exploration
> And the end of all our exploring
> Will be to arrive where we started
> And know the place for the first time.[2]

I asked Tommy if he thought that these lines describe what the journey was all about.

"I don't think we see the real end until we let go of trying to understand what that is," Tommy said. "When we let go, the real end is something like having drawn back, but different than before. I need to be healed of my need to be healed, but there is more. The more is the Father's will. Somehow we unite with the Father's will without defining it. That is the tension. That is the mystery. We hold on to the notion that the Father's will is good, and the possibilities are limitless, and that there is nothing impossible to Him. It is not a capitulation to 'whatever will be will be,' but a glorious breakthrough to a place where everything may still look the same, but nothing is the same.

"There is no formula for getting to that place. It is a partnering with God in fear and trembling. The fear comes from being presumptuous enough to believe that we can actually partner with God in this life and know what pleases God. It is safer to passively surrender and say whatever happens is God's will. The moment we take an active role, we are in danger of missing God's will. So we end up in this tenuous but exciting dance where, in trembling, we attempt to stay in step with God. We actively surrender while engaging God on the basis of His promises. That is what I am trying to work out. The tendency is to be too active or too passive."

$\mathcal{F}$or $\mathcal{R}$eflection

"Let no one deceive you with empty words, for because of such things God's wrath comes on those who are disobedient. Therefore do not be partners with them" (Ephesians 5:6-7).

"Do not sell your soul to anything that requires undue maintenance." Can you remember a time when you personally came close to losing something of yourself by allowing someone else's voice to become your conscience?

How do you discern when seeking others for the resources to do those things that please God overshadows seeking God as the source of all things?

"Until now you have not asked for anything in my name. Ask and you will receive, and your joy will be complete" (John 16:24).

Tommy said, "I need to be healed of my need to be healed . . . ." How have you experienced the tension between wanting to believe God for an answer to prayer and wanting to will what God wills?

Chapter 10
"Raising the Knife"

The natural

must be turned into the spiritual

by sacrifice…

Oswald Chambers,
My Utmost for His Highest

Stories inform us, amuse us, incite us, and delight us. They tell us who we are. They define us. They bind us together in communities. Tommy had always been drawn to the stories of the Judeo-Christian community. The stories from Scripture shaped and molded Tommy's understanding of God, himself, and the world in which he lived. Many times over the past two years, ever since he had been diagnosed with ALS, Tommy had revisited the story of Abraham and Isaac.

"This coming Sunday we will dedicate the new chapel," Tommy said as we sat watching the last hummingbird of summer suck nectar from the showy red blossoms of the cannas surrounding his new sun porch. "It is a significant benchmark for me. Two years ago today, I was diagnosed with ALS. One year ago today, we broke ground for the chapel. I have turned over and over in my mind a name for it: Mount Moriah, the mountain that Abraham and Isaac climbed. So much connected with this chapel is symbolic for me. The stained glass window on the north side of the chapel is of Mount Moriah with Abraham and Isaac. When I look up at that window and see the sun shining through the colored pieces of glass depicting the total surrender of Abraham, the appearance of the angel and God providing the ram, I see a visual image for my journey.

"I am moving forward in faith that God will give me this next year. Maybe that is my way of climbing that mountain that Abraham climbed. Everything to this point has brought me to the base of that mountain.

"When God said to Abraham, '…Take your son, your only son, Isaac, whom you love, and go to the region of Moriah. Sacrifice him there as a burnt offering …' (Genesis 22:2), Abraham did not argue with God.

He had already given up his son Ishmael, the product of his own efforts to fulfill God's will. Isaac was now his only son, all that he had left. I seem to be about to climb that same mountain. I know there will be a knife-raising moment when I reach the pinnacle of this mountain. I don't dare climb this mountain unless I am fully ready to raise that knife and plunge it into my Isaac. There are so many Isaacs for me. One Isaac is the church. It may be that I have to let go of the church and not try to figure out how it will go on in my absence. My hope is that when I raise the knife, God will provide a ram in the thicket. When Abraham's son, Isaac, said to him, 'The fire and the wood are here…but where is the lamb for the burnt offering?' (Genesis 22:7), Abraham said that God Himself would provide the lamb for the burnt offering. The only way that Abraham could have bound his son to that altar and raised the knife over him was to have total trust in God and not in God's provision for a way out. Abraham didn't have a plan B. Did Abraham believe that God would give back his son Isaac, resurrect him from the dead? I think so. What I don't know is what God is going to do for me—that is until I raise that knife. When I raise that knife, though, I must be fully prepared to plunge it into Isaac.

"Abraham lifted the knife in faith, not hope. I think it had to be faith, a done deal for him. Abraham left Ur in hope and his hope vacillated for years, but there were moments of revelation when faith came alive. When Abraham took Isaac and climbed Mount Moriah, he had to be acting in faith. I don't get on an airplane and hope; I get on an airplane in faith. Otherwise, I wouldn't do it at all. I'm saved because God revealed Himself in Christ to me, and I have trusted that revelation and based my life on it. It's more than hope. It's my confident expectation, a continuous act of faith.

"How do faith, hope, and love interact? Because God is love, He will never disappoint those who live by faith. That is what pleases Him most. It is the pattern by which God partners with human beings. He gives us the ability to imagine or 'hope' our future with or without Him. If we choose to imagine or 'hope' our future in Him, then He is going to make Himself known to us. Our response is the beginning of faith. That faith is based on the belief that God is love and that He loves us personally.

"God revealed to Abraham that He is the God who brings that which is dead back to life. Sarah was beyond the years of childbearing. Yet God brought that which was dead back to life. She conceived a son—Isaac, the son of promise. When God asked Abraham to sacrifice the son of promise, Abraham had faith that God could bring that which was dead back to life. Abraham said to his servants, 'Stay here with the donkey while I and the boy go over there. We will worship and then we will come back to you' (Genesis 22:5). *We will come back to you.* What an amazing statement of faith! Abraham grabbed hold of the revelation that God could raise his son from the dead and believed it—and because he did, it pleased God.

"I want to go up this mountain in faith. I know that Abraham came to his knife-raising moment and was forever changed. He came down the mountain a different man. Because he believed God, he was willing to sacrifice everything. Abraham called that mountain 'The Lord Will Provide.' I want to believe that as I reach the pinnacle of the mountain, I will face my knife-raising moment in faith, believing that God will provide. Everything that I have believed and preached all these years is being tested."

Tommy's own story was being shaped and defined by the story of Abraham and Isaac. In it he found a metaphor for letting go—giving up all that had meaning for him. Tommy identified with Abraham. For him, the knife-raising moment was the test of faith, a test of actively letting go.

I have always loved this story and also experience it as part of my own, but I enter into it from another perspective. I identified with Isaac and read the story through his eyes. Isaac trusted his father. He allowed his father to bind him to the altar. His only question was, "But where is the lamb for the burnt offering?" If Abraham was a man of faith, Isaac was the son of faith. While Abraham's faith was one of taking action, raising the knife, Isaac's faith was one of actively remaining still, staying bound to the altar, totally submitting himself to what was to come.

Three and one-half years ago, my husband and I grasped for the stars. For years, my husband had dreamed of owning his own business. We decided to take a leap into the unknown. We opened a nature store on the west side of Indianapolis. Within two years, we were deeply in debt and all of our savings had been used to keep the doors open. We had done everything we knew to make this business work, and now we were facing the shame and humiliation of having failed. We were on the verge of bankruptcy. Like Isaac, all we could do was to remain on the altar and trust God as our creditors raised the knife over us.

Earlier, when Tommy and I had talked about the predicament that my husband and I were in, he said to me, "The grace God will have to give me to let go is the same grace God will give you to hang on."

That night, as I lay awake in bed mulling over Tommy's words, I thought about what different paths Tommy and I had taken. Yet they intersected at this place of faith: for Tommy, a place of letting go; for me, a place of hanging on.

Tommy was born into a believing family. He was raised in a home where he was loved and cherished. He loved God. He loved people, and he loved life. He had much to let go of. During one of our conversations, I asked him if, as a teenager, he ever rebelled. He responded, "My only rebellion was when I went to Vietnam. My father didn't want me to go, but I felt that I had a calling on my life, and I couldn't minister to people who were required to do something I wouldn't do." After Vietnam, Tommy went to law school and then seminary. He was a man of faith, focus, and integrity. He had a zest for living and passionately held onto every moment of every day as a gift from God.

My life was so different. I grew up in a home with an angry father and an emotionally absent mother. As a young adult, I wandered aimlessly through life with no sense of meaning or purpose. I had nothing to hang on to. Once I vowed that I would never believe in a God who could allow so much pain and suffering in the world and do nothing. While Tommy was in Vietnam, I was living out my vow, doing drugs and marching in protests against the Vietnam War. While Tommy went to law school and seminary, I went to a drug rehabilitation center. Afterwards, as a new Christian, I still fought feelings of desolation and meaninglessness, always wondering if I could survive even the next moment, let alone the next day. After many years of pain and suffering, my husband and I had finally built a life filled with hope for the future. Now it seemed that, with an impending bankruptcy, all of that was about to come under the knife. Old feelings were surfacing. Hanging on felt as impossible for me as letting go was for Tommy. He was right. Neither of us could survive without the gift of grace.

For Reflection

"Some time later God tested Abraham" (Genesis 22:1a).

Isaac was the son of promise, a good thing, and yet Abraham had to be fully prepared to plunge his knife into Isaac. How have you responded to God in a "knife-raising" moment?

Abraham's faith was tested by taking action, raising the knife. Isaac's faith was tested by actively remaining still, submitting to the knife. To what kind of faith has God called you?

Chapter 11
"To the Congregation"

$\mathcal{T}$he real fast of the preacher is not from food,

but rather from eloquence,

from impressiveness and exquisite diction,

from everything that might hinder

the gospel of God being presented.

Oswald Chambers,
My Utmost for His Highest

"Good morning," Sandy said, grasping the pulpit and looking out at all the familiar faces that made up the congregation of Northview Christian Life—a congregation that she had long been a part of. On this particular morning, however, she embraced it from a different perspective. She now stood behind the pulpit and addressed the congregation.

ALS had continued to systematically shut down Tommy's motor functioning. He was now wheeled into the sanctuary on Sunday mornings, his chair placed by the front row where his family sat, near the podium. Now that he was no longer able to walk to the pulpit or speak in a voice that could be heard from the pulpit, his wife Sandy would speak for him. Along with her newly acquired and ever growing responsibilities for Tommy's care, Sandy had sat for hours, listening to Tommy as he dictated the words of his sermon to her. Then she painstakingly typed every word verbatim, and on this Sunday morning, she would read them to the congregation. Even on this bleak, gray day in January, the sanctuary was full, waiting in anticipation for words of encouragement from their pastor.

"I want to take this opportunity to present some of my husband's thoughts, since he is no longer able to stand in this pulpit himself," Sandy began.

"Tommy has asked me to preface this letter by telling you how he came to write it. Over the past twenty-seven months, he has gleaned insight from those who have shared their experiences of walking through difficult times with Christ. He has learned about suffering, fear, and abandonment. He has also learned about intimacy with Christ and God's grace in the midst of that suffering. There have been times when the struggles of those who are enduring such tests of faith have mirrored his own struggle. Many, like Abraham, who patiently endured years of waiting; David, who felt abandoned by God; the prophets, whose plaintive cries to the heavens seemingly turned to brass; and Jesus, who in the Garden of Gethsemane relinquished his will to that of the Father, have also taught him about suffering. Tommy has been drawn to the writings of faithful saints who down through the centuries have endured suffering as a great privilege: Saint John of the Cross, Thomas Aquinas, Oswald Chambers—the list could go on. The way they have lived their lives and the words they have spoken have been beacons in the midst of darkness.

"Last week, while reading Paul's letter to the Philippians, Tommy, like thousands before him, found himself living what Paul experienced while writing to the Philippians from prison. With a few changes, Tommy has taken the letter to the Philippians and rewritten it for you. He begins with this greeting:

> May God, our Father, and the Lord Jesus Christ, give you grace and peace. For over fifty years, I have squeezed every minute out of every day with a seemingly endless round of activity. Although I have been able to accomplish numerous goals and meet many expectations, I have not taken time to adequately reflect on those things that are important. I count my relationship with you and my love for you as one of life's dearest treasures. I think of you often, and when I do, I give thanks to God. I always pray for you, remembering that you have been partners in the good work of this church.
>
> Some of you have helped me share the good news from the beginning, and that has been over seventeen years. I am more sure than ever that what God began here will continue until it is finally finished on the day Jesus Christ comes back again.
>
> It is right for me to feel as I do about you, for you have a special place in my heart. Together we have shared the blessings of God, both when I was in good health, and now that I am sick. God knows how much I love you and long to be with you as I once was.
>
> Know that I am praying that your love for each other will

overflow, so that every need will be met with the same compassion that I have received, and that you will continue to grow in knowledge and understanding. More than ever, I want you to understand what really matters, so that you may live pure and blameless lives until Christ returns.

It is not enough just to be saved. Each of us must be filled with the fruit of our salvation—I am referring to those good things that are produced by having Jesus Christ in our lives.

I want you to know that everything that has happened to me these past two years has helped to spread the good news. Everyone in town, including government officials, community leaders, doctors, and neighbors, knows that it is my desire to bring glory to God in this trial. And because of my illness, many from this church and other Christians have gained confidence and become more bold in telling others about Christ. This makes me rejoice. For I know that as you pray for me and as the Holy Spirit helps me, this will all turn out for my deliverance. It is important that you understand that my conviction in this regard has not come by way of some dazzling revelation. Neither is it the posturing of someone who has refused to consider that it may not be God's will to heal me. My assurance is more that of the gentle persuasion of hearing God speak in dark and lonely places, in spite of every physical indication to the contrary. God has allowed me the grace to believe He is the one who brings that which is dead back to life!

In the meantime, I live in eager expectation and hope that I will in no way be ashamed, but that I will always be bold for Christ. I am often asked, "How should we pray for you?" Pray that my life will always honor Christ, whether I live or die.

Paul said it best. "For to me, to live is Christ and to die is gain" (Philippians 1:21). If I live, that means fruitful service for Christ. I'm torn between two desires: sometimes I want to live—that would be better for you; and sometimes I desire to depart and be with Christ—that would be far better for me.

I am convinced of this: it is better that I continue to be with you so that I can help you grow and experience the joy of the faith that I have discovered. Then, when I am healed, you will have even more reason to boast about what Jesus has done. But . . .

Sandy looked up from the pages; her eyes welled with tears, emotions flooding her face. "I'm sorry," she whispered into the silence of the congregation. Pulling her shoulders back and taking a deep breath, she began again.

But…whatever happens to me, you must live in a manner worthy of your calling. Then, whether I am healed or not, I can have the joy of knowing that you are fighting the good fight of faith.

Don't be intimidated by these uncertain times. Some will wonder whether or not the church can continue during my illness. I assure you that it will. God is demonstrating great confidence in this church by purifying our faith in this crucible. He has destined us to bring joy to Him in this way. This will be a sign to you that God is in control of everything, for we have been given not only the privilege of trusting in Christ, but also the privilege of suffering for him.

Some of you have asked, "Tommy, have you found any encouragement? Any comfort? Any fellowship in the Spirit?"

My answer is, "Yes!" I have seen how my affliction has drawn our church together. I see people wholeheartedly agreeing with each other, loving one another, and working together with one another.

God has answered my prayer—that we become a people whose unity is not based on a personality or a program, but on being a true community of Christ-Followers. With joy I have seen our church become that caring fellowship. If my suffering has helped to bring this to pass, then it has not been in vain.

Continue in humility, thinking of others as better than yourselves. In this way you are imitating our Lord. Though He was God, He did not demand and cling to His rights as God. He made Himself nothing, taking on the humble position of a slave, and in human form He obediently died a criminal's death on a cross.

This fact, that Christ would suffer such humiliation, has been a great source of comfort to me. I am consoled in each new loss knowing that Christ has experienced loss on an infinite scale. He identifies with me in my daily losses and struggles. When it seems as if I am being reduced to less and less, I know that Christ suffered the ultimate reduction. He laid aside His power and glory, confining Himself to a human body, a body that was stripped naked and nailed helplessly to a cross. I know He knows what I am going through.

Dearest friends, you have always been careful to follow my leadership when I could preach every week. Now that I am unable to preach, you must be careful to obey God's word. God is working in you, giving you the desire to obey Him and the power to do what pleases Him. Let me remind you again of those things you already know. You are to live clean, innocent lives, as children of God in a dark world. Just as this building has been set on a hill and cannot be hid, let your lives shine brightly in this community. Hold tightly to the Word of Life, so that when Christ returns, I will be proud of you, that my work was not useless. I commend to you the pastors who have worked beside me these many years. They genuinely care about your welfare. They have proven themselves faithful in caring for this flock and preaching the good news. They are gifted men and women who labor together with one heart and purpose. Afford them the respect worthy of their calling. Make their work among you pleasant by honoring them as the Lord's shepherds in your midst. I have given Jim, Gary, and John my full blessing to discharge the preaching ministry of this church during this time of waiting. Their lives and their love of God's word qualify them for this high calling.

Whatever happens…

Again Sandy paused before going on.

…may the Lord cause you to grow in understanding and grace. Not that I have already achieved these things, but I keep working towards that day when I will be all that Christ saved me to be. No, I am not there yet, but I am focusing all my energies on this one thing; forgetting the past and looking forward to what lies ahead, I strain to reach the end of the race and receive the prize for which God through Christ is calling me.

Dear brothers and sisters, I love you and long to be returned to you in perfect health, for you represent my life's work. Always be full of joy in the Lord. Again, rejoice. Don't worry about anything, but pray about everything.

And now may the God of all peace and hope bless you and be with you. Do not be afraid or discouraged for the battle is not yours. It is the Lord's. Be confident that nothing is impossible with Him, and He will not withhold any good thing from you.

Lovingly yours,
Tommy Paino

Silence, and then a deafening applause.

$\mathcal{F}$or $\mathcal{R}$eflection

"Dear friends, since God so loved us, we also ought to love one another" (1 John 4:11).

Tommy said that the people of Northview Christian Life were becoming a people whose unity was not based on a personality or a program, but on being a true community of Christ-followers. Do you believe that you are part of such a community? Why or why not?

What can you do to help create or perpetuate such a community?

Chapter 12
"Beckoning to the Bridge"

*I*t is going to cost the natural in you everything,

not something.

Oswald Chambers,
My Utmost for His Highest

It was February 1998. By this time, Northview Christian Life had become known as the church whose pastor had Lou Gehrig's disease, the very thing that Tommy had hoped to avoid. Tommy was known throughout the community of Carmel, the Assemblies of God Church at large, and even in remote parts of the world. People were praying for him. People were watching him. If Tommy could beat this, if he were healed, maybe they, too, could believe in his kind of God. But if the Lord chose to take him, they would have to reassess their understanding of a God who allows the righteous to die. Tommy received gifts, cards, and letters. In fact, his postpersons were well acquainted with the Paino mailbox. Gifts, cards, letters, and special deliveries were delivered to the Paino household by the bagful. He received unsolicited and solicited advice. He received books, pamphlets, paraphernalia, as well as all the expectations that went with them.

There were also those who knew that Tommy and I were working on this book. One friend called me and in passing said, "Oh, by the way, have you read *Tuesdays with Morrie?*" I hadn't even heard of *Tuesdays with Morrie* but I immediately went to the bookstore and bought a copy. As soon as I finished reading it, I bought a second copy for Tommy.

That week, after reading the book, Tommy spoke these words to his wife, Sandy. On Sunday morning, Sandy again stood at the podium and read Tommy's message to the congregation.

Time and words have become precious commodities, and I don't have the strength or time for unnecessary thoughts. The past number of weeks has presented an intensifying attack on my peace of mind. I understand what David meant by the "terror that stalks by night." These times of terror for me are short in duration, even though they seem much longer. I repeat God's Word over and over again and praise Him in the face of overwhelming darkness. My degenerating physical condition is obvious to all. I am especially grieved by my inability to speak. When you talk to me, look for my answer in my eyes. Even though my body is failing, my spiritual life is thriving during this time of testing. Weakness in every other area is compensated for by the ever-increasing strength of my inner man. My hope is in God's promises, my faith is that God is speaking a living word for this circumstance, and my love is anchored in a God who does all things well.

Recently, I was given a book written by Mitch Albom titled *Tuesdays with Morrie*. This book chronicles the last weeks of a man dying of ALS. Morrie Schwartz, a college professor who contracted ALS when he was seventy, had been a source of wisdom and guidance for the author, Mitch Albom, during his youth. The book is an account of the conversations about life and death between the two men on the last fourteen Tuesdays of Morrie's life. In a compelling passage, Morrie describes his experience like this:

> ALS is like a lit candle: it melts your nerves and leaves your body a pile of wax....By the end, if you are still alive, you are breathing through a tube in a hole in your throat, while your soul, perfectly awake, is imprisoned inside a lime husk, perhaps able to blink, or cluck a tongue, like something from a science fiction movie, the man frozen inside his own flesh.[1]

Over the past few years, I have often wondered why the general public is often captivated by those suffering from this disease. At first, I thought it was the curiosity that prompts us to wonder whether or not we would have the courage to face such a trial with grace and dignity. But I have come to believe it's far more than that. I now think the progressive, unrelenting, and inevitable outcome provides a rare glimpse of someone making the transition from this life to the next. Morrie Schwartz came to the same realization. In an early conversation with Mitch Albom he states the same thought, "Here's the thing, ...People see me as a bridge. I'm not as alive as I used to be, but I'm not yet dead. I'm sort of...in-between.... I'm on the last great journey here—and people want me to tell them what to pack." It's as if we are observing someone on a bridge between this world and the next. We are drawn near to see how we should pack our suitcase for eternal life.

I am increasingly aware of your intense scrutiny of my faith. I welcome you to come near and learn from my experience.

This morning I want to draw your attention to some familiar words of Jesus. You will immediately recognize them as the first two sentences of the Lord's Prayer. Matthew 6:9-10 reads as follows:

> ...Our Father in heaven,
> hallowed be your name,
> your kingdom come,
> your will be done
> on earth as it is in heaven.

These passages imply God's active participation in the affairs of human beings. There is a plan in God's mind for His world, just as there is in heaven. In some marvelous way we have been invited into the grand purposes of God Himself. God has initiated a movement on this insignificant planet.

A movement is the conviction that the future can be created, not simply experienced or endured. Many people will never know the joy of being part of some grand movement. God's intent for us as a church is that we be a people shaping the future here on this earth in line with that which is in heaven.

Our church stands at an exciting fork in the road. One path leads to becoming a successful organization. Our facilities are in place, talented and gifted leadership is on call, and programs are functioning to meet almost every need. Successful organizations can and do accomplish much good. But, even the most worthwhile organizations cannot fulfill our God-given potential. Something in all of us yearns to be part of more than an organization. We long to be part of something that sees the future as something to be created rather than simply experienced. In other words, we want to be part of God's movement on this planet.

This is the other road. It beckons us towards realizing our potential of being part of God's movement here on earth. It leads us towards realizing that God's will is being accomplished here, just as it is being accomplished in heaven. As I stand on this bridge between heaven and earth, I can see that doing the business of God's kingdom is what matters most. I can also see how many things compete with and confuse the movement of God's kingdom. Let me be as clear as possible in explaining how this works.

God's kingdom is nothing more and nothing less than being formed into the image of Christ. All other endeavors fall somewhere short of the point. This is God's will for your life and the life of our church. He is not impressed by our building, our efforts to evangelize the world, or the excellence of our ministries. He is not taken in by the charisma of our leaders or our standing in this community. He is concerned that we become like Christ.

Because so many things compete with and confuse this movement of God's spirit in our lives and the life of our church, our calling will constantly be tested. Because our tendency is to organize our lives around good but lesser things, God will test and refine that which is not of His kingdom. We should not think it strange when fiery trials come our way. We must know that they are intended to keep us focused on that which is eternal. Testing is never pleasant, but it always promises to yield eternal benefits.

God allows times of testing for three kingdom reasons: first, to teach us to trust God; second, to build Christ-like character in us; and third, to further God's purposes among us. I believe that we are experiencing a season of testing. Let us be confident that God is drawing us into a closer relationship with Him. He is building Christ-like character in us, and He is working His purposes through us.

Testing also gives us an opportunity to check our suitcase. As one standing on the bridge, suitcase in hand, I'm taking special inventory of my baggage. It has never been more important for me to carry kingdom items only. Come close and examine my suitcase. I have already discarded a number of things that I had been carrying for some time. There are more things that have to go, but for now, I'm still hanging onto them. Come even closer, and see how light I'm beginning to travel. I have been left with humility. This was not something that I expected in my youth or in the flower of my strength. Now, I cherish it as the most Christ-like feature of all. Even now, it is hard to verbalize it, because to even mention it in connection with my life causes it to evaporate. Pride is a constant enemy of Christ-like humility and surfaces again and again. Maybe my daily routine of constant dependence on others has been a special grace in working a spirit of humility in me. Jesus says, "Blessed are the poor in spirit..." (Matthew 5:3). These words were spoken by one who suffered the ultimate humiliation. In the only text where Jesus describes Himself; He says, "...for I am gentle and humble in heart..." (Matthew 11:29). If we would follow Christ's example and humble ourselves before God and others, then God can raise us up as effective servants in His kingdom. I am also carrying another strange item, a deep spirit of sorrow and grief. In recent weeks, I have experienced anxiety attacks. For those who have walked this path, I need say no more. Thankfully, most of you have had no experience with the kind of fear that I'm about to describe. It is a dreadful state of mind and spirit so dark that seemingly no amount of light can penetrate it. This condition defies rational explanation. It is a slithering dragon of terror that resides at the core of the human soul. Unannounced, it rises from the murky depths of our souls and attempts to steal the last vestiges of our trust in a God who loves us personally. It is the terror that under this veneer of human existence there lies a deep bottomless pit, that ultimately our existence has no meaning beyond this thread of time and space that we now occupy. In recent weeks, with pounding heart and sweaty palms, I have faced this demon on several occasions. When locked in battle with this enemy, what lasts only a few minutes seems like an eternity.

This experience has given me new insight into the human condition. It has expanded my capacity for compassion beyond anything I had known before. I now understand why we so desperately seek any diversion that will prevent us from contact with this core fear of the human soul. No wonder Jesus looked over Jerusalem and wept. My heart now mourns when I see the futile attempts that we all make in the hope of adding meaning to our lives. Our status symbols, our attempts at control, our quests for amusement are all hollow attempts to cover this fear that dogs us by day and this terror that stalks us by night. As Christians, we are called to grieve the desperate condition of the world around us. Like our Lord, we must be a people of sorrows, well acquainted with grief. Perhaps this perspective on life cannot become reality until we are standing on the bridge.

Finally, I am packing spiritual brokenness. Like humility and mourning, this also appears to be a peculiar item. For me, brokenness means releasing my need to be in control. How strange it is to have spent a lifetime grasping for control, only to discover that I cannot carry it across the bridge. Now I see that God has been trying to relieve me of this burden for a very long time. I was simply too dense to know it. Brokenness is the pathway to every spiritual blessing. It is in brokenness that we are emptied of self and filled with God. I think the Biblical word for brokenness is meekness. "Blessed are the meek, for they will inherit the earth" (Matthew 5:5).

We will never attain spiritual maturity until we are broken. In the book *Stepping Heavenward,* the author tells of her experience with an elderly saint who was on her deathbed. The author asked this dear woman what she conceived to be the characteristics of an advanced state of grace. Listen to this elderly saint's answer.

> ...I think that the mature Christian is...what he was
> in his best moments in the progressive stages of his life.
> There were seasons, all along his course, when he loved
> God supremely; when he embraced the cross joyfully and
> penitently; when he held intimate communion with Christ
> and loved his neighbor as himself. But he was always in
> terror lest under the force of temptation all this should
> give place to deadness and dullness, when he would chafe
> and rebel in the hour of trial and judge his fellowman with
> a harsh and bitter judgement and give way to angry pas-
> sionate emotions. But these fluctuations cease, after a time,
> to disturb his peace. Love to Christ becomes the abiding,
> inmost principle of his life; he loves Him rather for what
> He is than for what He has done or will do for him indi-
> vidually, and God's honor becomes so dear to him that he
> feels personally wounded when that is called in question.
> And the will of God becomes so dear to him that he loves
> it best when it "triumphs at his cost."
>
> Once he only prayed at times and seasons and idolized
> good frames and fervent emotions. Now he prays without
> ceasing, and whether on the mount or down in the depths
> depends wholly upon his Savior.
>
> His old self-confidence has now given place to child-
> like humility that will not let him take a step alone; and the
> sweet peace that is now habitual to him, combined with
> the sense of his own imperfections, fills him with love for
> his fellowman. He hears and believes and hopes and en-
> dures all things and thinketh no evil. The tones of his
> voice, the very expression of his countenance become
> changed, love now controlling where human passions held
> full sway. In short, he is not only a new creature in Jesus
> Christ, but has the habitual and blessed consciousness that
> this is so.[2]

These are the words of someone standing on the bridge between two worlds. And here's the punch line: all of us who have put our faith in Jesus Christ are standing on that bridge. Once we trust in Him, our perspective changes. We are swept into the movement of God's kingdom. As a part of that movement, we embrace humility, mourning, and brokenness—and our hunger for righteousness is filled by God Himself.

Tommy's words, like clean laundry hung out to blow in the breeze on a crisp warm day, hung in the air as Sandy stepped away from the podium. Times of testing had knocked on Tommy's door. He was checking his suitcase in front of a thousand people. Would he be able to let go of all that belonged to this world and carry only those items that belonged to the kingdom of God? Sometimes God heals our bodies and sometimes He anoints our bodies and our brokenness for His purposes. Each Sunday, the congregation came together, watching, waiting, and praying. If they could see God actively in the midst of Tommy's suffering, perhaps they could believe that God would be in the midst of what was to come for them, too.

$\mathcal{F}$or $\mathcal{R}$eflection

"He causes his sun to rise on the evil and the good, and sends rain on the righteous and the unrighteous" (Matthew 5:45b).

Tommy's condition brought up thought-provoking questions for his church family. If God allows the righteous to die, then why should any of us pray for healing?

"For no one can lay any foundation other than the one already laid, which is Jesus Christ. If any man builds on this foundation using gold, silver, costly stones, wood, hay or straw, his work will be shown for what it is, because the Day will bring it to light. It will be revealed with fire, and the fire will test the quality of each man's work" (I Corinthians 3:11-13).

"God allows times of testing for three kingdom reasons: first, to teach us to trust God; second, to build Christ-like character in us; and third, to further God's purposes among us." As you look back on times of testing in your own life, what do you believe God's purposes were for you?

123

Chapter 13
"The Mystery of Healing"

$\mathcal{W}$e are not here to prove God answers prayer;

we are here to be living monuments of God's grace.

Oswald Chambers,
My Utmost for His Highest

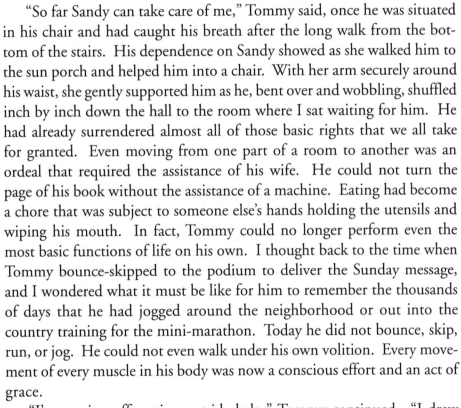

"So far Sandy can take care of me," Tommy said, once he was situated in his chair and had caught his breath after the long walk from the bottom of the stairs. His dependence on Sandy showed as she walked him to the sun porch and helped him into a chair. With her arm securely around his waist, she gently supported him as he, bent over and wobbling, shuffled inch by inch down the hall to the room where I sat waiting for him. He had already surrendered almost all of those basic rights that we all take for granted. Even moving from one part of a room to another was an ordeal that required the assistance of his wife. He could not turn the page of his book without the assistance of a machine. Eating had become a chore that was subject to someone else's hands holding the utensils and wiping his mouth. In fact, Tommy could no longer perform even the most basic functions of life on his own. I thought back to the time when Tommy bounce-skipped to the podium to deliver the Sunday message, and I wondered what it must be like for him to remember the thousands of days that he had jogged around the neighborhood or out into the country training for the mini-marathon. Today he did not bounce, skip, run, or jog. He could not even walk under his own volition. Every movement of every muscle in his body was now a conscious effort and an act of grace.

"I'm putting off getting outside help," Tommy continued. "I draw these lines and then put off crossing them. This tension between fighting and resting is one that I keep coming back to. On the one hand, there are those who would say that the outcome of this disease is inevitable, so why fight it? But that doesn't work for me. On the other hand, I know that fighting it takes so much energy and sets me up for constant disappointment. I am trying to hold this tension. I'm expecting God to give me a revelation or insight to help me navigate these murky waters between fighting and resting. I think it has to do with the mystery of what God is doing. I believe God can heal me and I wouldn't want to let go of that hope. Many who are praying for me believe that this is exactly what God wills for me, my total and complete physical healing. Nevertheless, for me it is a struggle between believing God heals and letting God be God. The trick is to ultimately will what God wills. It's just that I don't know what that looks like yet.

"If God were to heal me, every move would become a living sacrifice. Most of us live our lives by our convictions, creeds, and doctrines about who or what we think God is, oblivious to God's moment-by-moment sustaining grace. We have to reach the place where our convictions, creeds, and doctrines no longer matter. We stop talking about God and enter into communion with the God who sustains us. I don't have to be whole physically to know God in that way.

"I am almost at the point where I would like to preach a sermon on healing. I am not sure if I am ready, even now, because of where I am physically. I know what everyone wants to hear. I'm afraid that once I get the snowball rolling down the hill, everyone will want to run with it, but they will want to run in different directions. I have intentionally made only bleak references to healing since my diagnosis. I want to address it head on, but it is fraught with danger for both the church and me.

"I believe that there are several stages to this process of believing God for healing. The first three stages are summed up in emptying, abandoning, and accepting. We empty ourselves of our preconceived notions of what God will do. We abandon our own desire to be healed, and we accept what God wills. This is the side of faith that lets go and sees beyond what is visible.

It is what comes next that is dangerous to preach. It is believing God for the miracle now. Whenever you preach from this place, it is tempting to only see the miracle as God's provision and not all the other possibilities. What is difficult to discern is how to know when you have drained the cup—in all its bitterness, because in some ways there seems to be no end to that. There's always more to die to; more to be surrendered. I think the secret is to recognize that we will never reach the place of total surrender but must continually will to surrender. It is easy for me in my own thinking to believe that I have traveled that distance and arrived at that place, but I know in my heart that that is not true.

"An interesting series of experiences happened this weekend that has caused me to ponder these things. Last Saturday night, a young woman stopped by our house. She has had a spiritual awakening of sorts. She had just come from a camp meeting in Columbus, Ohio, where she had heard a charismatic, 'rising star' evangelist speak. She was so excited about what she had heard that she wanted to tell us about it. The next morning in church, another young woman who had also been to this camp meeting almost accosted me after the first service, insisting that God had told her to speak with me between services. Later, Sunday evening, I was flipping through the channels on the television when I came to a program with the same young 'rising star' evangelist that these two young women had both gone to hear, preaching a 'name-it-and-claim-it' faith message. His presentation of the 'name-it-and-claim-it' faith teaching was more articulate than any that I have ever heard. The long and the short of his message was this: Faith is the dynamic principle operating in the realm of the unseen. It is the power that supersedes all other powers. He equated faith with God. After an hour-and-one-half of preaching, he concluded by saying that we have the authority to name and claim God's promises into existence.

"My struggle with this kind of teaching is that there is always a temptation to use our God-given authority to manipulate the dynamic of faith or to claim God's promises for our own ends. Everything that this evangelist said was true, but there is another dynamic at play here. At some point, we have to experience brokenness, a willingness to relinquish our desires in trust and obedience to the One who is the Promise. Here is the ultimate irony. In the end, the very thing that was being espoused by this young evangelist is ours and does come to us, but in a different way. There is a time of testing that comes first; otherwise, we don't own our faith. When Abraham climbed Mount Moriah with his son Isaac, he didn't know whether God would take his son's life or give his son back to him. He went up that mountain in faith, trusting God for the outcome. The same was true for Moses. Moses climbed the mountain and God showed him the promise, but then God took his life. Here is the ultimate symbol of the cross. When Jesus set out for Jerusalem, knowing the road led to Golgotha, His faith was in His Father, not in avoiding the suffering of the cross.

"The longer I walk this path, the fewer conclusions I have. I know God can heal, which begs the question, 'Does God heal?' Scripture is clear on that point. It is God's nature to heal—Jehovah Rapha, 'the God who heals.' But the question, 'Does God heal?' is not the fundamental question. The critical question is 'Does God hear and answer prayer?' It is that question that moves us to our true vocation as a Christian, that of prayer. The purpose of prayer is to produce a life in communion with Christ. Healing is the byproduct of a life given to prayer. The difficulty for most of us is that even though we may have accepted that our vocation as a Christian is prayer, we still focus on getting specific answers to our prayers rather than Jesus, who is the Answer to all prayer.

"For those who have entered this life of prayer, God gives the 'Aha.' 'Ahas' are words of life that support our faith—words of healing, such as 'this is not unto death.' But we can't seek those words. We have to seek the Giver of the words. More often than not we seek relief and answers and miss the real meaning of prayer—communion with God the Father.

"I've never quite known what to do with 'words' given to me from others as 'thus saith the Lord.' Sometimes they are born out of the person's love for me, and at other times they are born out of the person's neediness. That is why it is especially hard to hear a word from someone who is close to me. Often love and closeness become a distraction. I am more attuned to words that come from unexpected sources."

"Tommy," I interjected, "when you say that the critical question is not 'Does God heal?' but 'Does God hear and answer prayer?' there are those who might think that you are taking the easy way out by not stating that you do or do not believe that God will heal you personally."

Tommy paused for a moment. "I am heading towards resolve, a growing persuasion. I have an inclination that God is doing something very good. Even in saying that, I am cautious—not lacking in faith. I am aware of how many people are watching and I don't want to err on either side.

"I was stuck for a long time, reluctant to even consider a healing intervention. 'Why would God heal me and not heal someone else?' Oddly, I joined the army during Vietnam for almost the same reason. I asked myself, 'Why should I be exempt because I can get an educational deferment, when some guy in the ghetto has no choice but to accept being drafted?' At that time, I had no idea as to what the war was about and could not have cared less. 'Why should I, because of some privilege, be exempt?' I feel the same way about healing. 'Why should I, because of some divine privilege, be exempt?'

"God the Father has gently reminded me that these matters are in His hands. I have to accept what He has in mind. I'm telling Him it's okay either way."

For Reflection

"Fight the good fight of the faith . . ." (I Timothy 6:12a).

"This is what the Lord says: 'Stand at the crossroads and look; ask for the ancient paths, ask where the good way is, and walk in it, and you will find rest for your souls . . .'" (Jeremiah 6:16a).

Tommy struggled with the tension between fighting and resting. What issues in your own life have left you in this tension between fighting and resting?

How was this tension resolved for you?

"He himself bore our sins in his body on the tree, so that we might die to sins and live for righteousness; by his wounds you have been healed" (I Peter 2:24).

Knowing that God heals, and yet knowing that even good and faithful men and women are not always healed, what does it mean to ultimately will what God wills in regards to healing?

Tommy said that most of us pray to God in hopes of receiving relief and answers. If you believe that the real meaning of prayer is communion with God the Father, how does that affect the way you pray?

Chapter 14
"Trembling on Holy Ground"

*L*et the past sleep,

but let it sleep on the bosom of Christ,

and go out into the irresistible future with Him.

Never let the sense of failure corrupt your new action.

Oswald Chambers,
My Utmost for His Highest

Every year I heard the pastors and staff talking about it in the office. It was always spoken of with great anticipation and excitement, but also with a degree of secrecy. There were lots of meetings for planning and more meetings for praying that surrounded the event. Hundreds of members in the church and many from other churches were a part of this grand occasion. Even my clients would talk to me about how it had been a transforming event in their lives. Realizing that they were revealing a precious secret, they would stop and say something like, "Oh, but you haven't gone yet. I really shouldn't talk with you about this." Trays of cookies and brownies, bags of chips and M & Ms, containers with pies and cakes—more food than I had ever seen in one place at one time—began showing up in the church kitchen a day or two before it was to happen, always marked with the words, "Do not eat. Discipleship Walk."

It wasn't the intrigue, the gentle nudging by pastors and friends, or even my own sense that this would be a good thing to do for myself spiritually that prompted me to go on the Discipleship Walk. It was having gone three years without a vacation and collapsing into total exhaustion that finally got to me. I needed this four-day, three-night retreat with no responsibilities and lots of chocolate, cookies, and pies.

Tommy and a few other members of the church had initiated the first Discipleship Walk some years back. I knew that it had been a life-changing experience for many that had already gone before me. I went with the sense that, at least for me, it would be an opportunity to rest from the responsibilities and stresses of my day-to-day existence. To my amazement, it turned out to be a rite of passage into a new dimension spiritually. I found myself trembling on holy ground.

"Tommy," I said with excitement as I entered his room. "Everything you said about the Discipleship Walk is true. It was one of the most extraordinary experiences I have ever had. During a time of praise on the second day, we sang the song, 'I Will Change Your Name.' Let me see if I can remember the words for you. Don't worry, Tommy, I won't attempt to sing them.

I will change your name
You shall no longer be called
Wounded, Outcast
Lonely or Afraid

I will change your name
Your new name shall be
Confidence, Joyfulness
Overcoming One

Faithfulness, Friend of God
One Who Seeks my Face [1]

"I knew when I went on the walk that I was exhausted and probably more susceptible to tears than usual, but when we sang the word, 'Confidence,' I began to feel such grief, a floodgate of tears began to gush forth. I couldn't stop crying, and I didn't understand why. The next day, during a time of prayer, the Lord revealed to me that because of what had happened six years ago, I had lost my confidence, and for the last six years I had been trying to earn back His favor.

"Do you remember the Stantons, a couple that you referred to me for marriage counseling?"

The question was rhetorical. I knew Tommy had not forgotten what had happened six years ago. He was the one who had referred Richard and Mary to me for counseling. There had been some incidents of violence, and Mary was afraid of her husband, Richard. After a few sessions together, I began seeing them separately. She moved out of the house and got a restraining order against Richard. At my insistence, he went into a program for men who had battered their spouses. It was on a Friday morning after he had completed the twenty-two week program that he came back into my office and announced that he had done everything that I had told him to do, and now he was going to go and do right by his wife. A cold chill went through me as he stood up to walk out of the office. I couldn't hug him or shake his hand as he left. I knew something was different about him, but it was only a premonition. There was nothing that he had said or done that directly supported my sense about him. Later in the afternoon, I received word that Richard had gone to his wife's house and shot and killed her; and when the police caught up with him, he put the barrel of the gun to his own head and pulled the trigger.

For months I walked around in a daze, replaying the events of that Friday morning. What if I had asked Richard specifically what it was that he intended to do? Could I have done something to stop him? The questions haunted me day and night. In Ecclesiastes the Quester, David's son and king in Jerusalem, concluded that "brutality stupefies even the wise and destroys the strongest heart" (Ecclesiastes 7:7, The Message). Even these words of wisdom from Scripture did not comfort me. Eventually I discovered that if I worked harder and longer, the activity drowned out the questions during the day; and at night, out of sheer exhaustion, I could sleep.

"Tommy, this is the first time since Richard murdered his wife and committed suicide that I have felt at peace with myself and at peace with God. The Discipleship Walk provided an opportunity for me to create a space for God to occupy. As I began to slow down, I was able to commune with God again. I had almost forgotten how. In that place of care and prayer, God gave me back my confidence. I was on holy ground."

Tommy listened with furrowed brow. After an appropriate period of time, he responded. "About ten years ago, a young woman in our church committed suicide. I had been counseling her prior to her death. Her mother, who was from another denomination, in her own pain at the loss of her daughter, blamed me for her daughter's death. Three years later, I signed up to go on what the Episcopalians call a Cursillo Walk. It is similar to the Emmaus Walk in the Methodist Church and the Discipleship Walk that you just experienced. My motivation for attending the Cursillo Walk was to use it as a prototype for developing a similar retreat for our community. My initial experience on that retreat was the springboard for our Discipleship Walk.

"When I arrived at the retreat center where the walk was to be held, you can't imagine my surprise when I discovered that this mother who had so berated me after the death of her daughter was the only other non-Episcopalian on this walk. Immediately, I went to the lay director and offered to leave rather than be an offense to her, possibly harming her ability to receive from God on that particular weekend. After much discussion and prayer, the lay director said that he believed it was no coincidence that we both signed up for this walk on this particular weekend. In fact, he believed that God intended this to happen for the purpose of restoration and healing. The lay director talked with the woman and she agreed to stay also. Over the next two days we chanced to connect and talk and cry through that experience of her daughter's suicide. It was a healing time for both of us. It showed me how God can providentially arrange circumstances to bring about healing. I came away from the Cursillo Walk knowing that I wanted to offer a retreat weekend where members from our congregation would have opportunities for that kind of healing experience. I think if there is any one thing that I have done right, it has to be the Discipleship Walk."

I had never heard the story about the young woman who had committed suicide and how God had providentially brought healing to both Tommy and the young woman's mother. I felt at peace with myself, at peace with God, and a bond with Tommy. I was in awe at how, by God's providential hand, our paths had crisscrossed through our mutual sense of failure to heal another and God's provision of a retreat weekend to heal us. Yes, if I were to point to one particular thing that Tommy has done right, it would be the Discipleship Walk.

For Reflection

"For it is by grace you have been saved, through faith—and this not from yourselves, it is the gift of God—not by works, so that no one can boast" (Ephesians 2:8-9).

The author, in trying to make sense of a crazy making event in her life, had seen herself as having failed God and attempted to earn back God's favor. Have there been times in your own life when you have worked to earn God's approval or attempted to earn back God's favor?

"Be still and know that I am God . . ." (Psalm 46:10*a*).

When the author was able to create a space for God, she was able to commune with God again. With the ever increasing pace of modern-day existence, how do you create space for God to enter in?

Chapter 15
"Good Friday"

$\mathcal{T}$he Spirit of God

in the process of sanctification

will strip me until I am nothing but "myself,"

that is the place of death.

Oswald Chambers,
My Utmost for His Highest

Catastrophic loss grinds up our souls and spits them back to us as sawdust. Metaphors, symbols, parables, and analogies help us make sense of, name, and define our experiences when we are blind-sided by catastrophe. Each year, for example, thousands of individuals visit the Holocaust Museum in an effort to bring sanity to an unbelievably insane event, the murder of six million Jews. If we can understand suffering and pain of that magnitude, then perhaps we can have hope in the midst of our own infinitesimal, though seemingly intolerable, suffering.

Tommy sought to understand and make peace with his own pain. He read books, looking for metaphors, parables, and words to describe his own experience. One such book that gave him words for his experience was *A Grace Disguised*. Gerald Sittsler, the author, was a man pressed to the limit, face-to-face with utterly devastating suffering. A tragic accident had claimed three generations of his family: his mother, his wife, and his young daughter. Plunged into a darkness that left him unsure if he would ever again emerge sane, normal, or believing, the author begins to describe his experience.

In the hours that followed the accident, the initial shock gave way to an unspeakable agony. I felt dizzy with grief's vertigo, cut off from family and friends, tormented by the loss, nauseous from the pain. After arriving at the hospital, I paced the floor like a caged animal, only recently captured. I was so bewildered that I was unable to voice questions or think rationally. I felt wild with fear and agitation, as if I was being stalked by some deranged killer from whom I could not escape. I could not stop crying. I could not silence the deafening noise of crunching metal, scream-ing sirens, and wailing children. I could not rid my eyes of the vision of violence, of shattering glass and shattered bodies. All I wanted was to be dead. Only the sense of responsibility for my three surviving children and the habit of living for forty years kept me alive.[1]

"This man walks through his experience in a way that almost parallels everything that I have thought and felt over the past two and one-half years, down to the way he chooses to embrace his darkness," Tommy said in response to having read the book. "The author in describing his own agony describes my emotions since being told that I have ALS. I like what he says about suffering. We cannot compare one person's suffering with another person's suffering. The more I walk this path, the more I realize that I am not unique. This path has been traveled many times by many people."

It was Good Friday of 1998. Tommy and I had met weekly for almost a year now. At first we met in his office at the church. There we discussed the books that we both had read and what the writing of this book would achieve. When Tommy was no longer able to go to the office, we moved our discussions to the sun porch at the back of his house. It is a cozy, warm room surrounded by cottage flowers and pine trees. In the fall we watched the last hummingbirds of summer drinking enough nectar from the tall red cannas to sustain them for their long flight south. There we discussed family, church, suffering, loss, letting go, loneliness, and heal-ing. Occasionally we would touch on death and the meaning of the resurrection.

Today, I sat in a small blue chair near the bed in Tommy's bedroom. Tommy, covered with a white quilt and his head propped to one side with a pillow, continued.

"I'm trying to dispel denial on my part, but I don't want to be fatalis-tic. I think that one has to move through a trial, and look back to analyze what it is about. In the beginning, I was in a perpetual state of anxiety. With each new loss, there was an underlying sense of dread of what was to come. I was hit with overwhelming waves of fear. How would I cope with the next wave? That has all changed. I still experience a consistent parade of losses. The losses are more final, but I'm no longer in denial. Early on I learned to adjust. I learned new ways to dress myself, new ways to walk. At long last I have become weary of the long procession of losses. There is almost a sense of relief. I think I am moving towards resolve, but I may still be too close to what is happening to me to know for sure. I'm not in a position to make conclusive statements about anything. The further down this road I travel, the fewer answers I have. There is this overwhelming sense that there is so much more for me to learn. That is why I am still reluctant to put anything into print yet. I wish I had journaled my feelings in the beginning, but they were too sharp and con-fusing, and I didn't have the psychic energy to wade into all of that then.

"I am preparing a sermon for Sandy to read to the congregation on Easter Sunday. This may be the last time that I can do this. The chal-lenge is to see the resurrection in a new light. I want to tell the story from this unique perspective. I think I will be walking a tightrope, because it is hard to address the resurrection without talking about death. (The Chris-tian hope is not in healing, but in resurrection, which is something entirely different.) One has to die to experience resurrection. So the dark side of Easter is the infallibility of death. Easter is really a funeral message—which only recently occurred to me. I've preached scores of funerals, but I never made that connection before. I think the difference is the atmo-sphere. We send one message with the coffin and another with the songs of triumph sung by the choir on Easter morning. I may refer to that dualism. The good news is that the message will be short." Tommy smiled as he spoke of his increasing difficulty to talk for any extended period of time.

"Tommy, do you need anything else before I leave?" Sandy asked, peering in the door.

"No, I'll be all right," he answered. "Sandy has become the switch-board for our family. It's as if I'm not here at times. I don't think it is intentional. I notice that people are taking time to stop by and express their feelings about me. I think it is their way of saying 'Goodbye.' I'm mostly busy processing my own journey.

"I have done a ton of work in dying to everything. I am sensing that

God is moving me to a new place. To simply die to things can't be the goal. It has to be the means to some greater end. That's the surprise. What I don't know is whether my process of dying will open some door to service or if it is my ticket through the gates into eternity.

"The danger of living this crucified life is to lose sight of God's grace. Introducing grace into the mix is essential or it becomes a gospel of works. There's no formula to reconcile these seemingly opposing concepts. My limited experience tells me that we are to follow the way of the cross, but then at some unknown point we collapse into God's grace. We can't truly collapse into God's grace without first following the way of the cross. To do so would be to cheapen grace. When I am around those who tout grace, I want to say, 'But what about the cross?' And when I am around those who carry the cross, I want to say, 'But what about grace?'

"On the one hand, we are to seek out and walk the narrow path. And on the other, we are to embrace those who are seemingly walking the broader path. Those who have chosen to walk the narrow path are the very ones who should reach out to the vilest of sinners and extend grace. (Too often the opposite occurs.) In my opinion this is the essence of the Gospel. I'll never resolve that mystery."

Tommy had been pressed to the limit, plunged into darkness, stalked by a deranged killer ALS. In the beginning, the seepage of pain that comes with grief permeated every crack and crevice of his soul. Paula D'Arcy, a woman who lost her husband and child in a fatal accident, echoed the same feelings that Tommy—as well as all of those who are catapulted into agony—experienced. In *Gift of the Red Bird*, she writes, "I blink my eyes and all I love is gone…It feels as if someone has hurled a hot brick against my chest and my hands cannot take it off.… I cry because my hand is so small and the wave so powerful."[2] Tommy, like D'Arcy and Sittsler, had been cut through to the bone. He was no longer in control. There were no more distractions. There were no more illusions. He could find words and metaphors in the sufferings of others that helped him define his own experience of suffering, but the words he had always used to define his experience of God now seemed narrow and too absolute. As Tommy plunged headfirst into the waters of "dying," his message took on new life. Tommy had always had a message. He had been an eloquent preacher. His words were always uplifting, Biblically based, and grace-filled. But as Tommy plunged into unknown waters, he found himself face to face with a greater Mystery: the fewer the words, the greater the revelation of the nature of God.

For Reflection

"Therefore, my dear friends, as you have always obeyed—not only in my presence, but now much more in my absence—continue to work out your salvation with fear and trembling, for it is God who works in you to will and to act according to his good purpose" (Philippians 2:12-13).

"And if by grace, then it is no longer by works; if it were, grace would no longer be grace" (Romans 11:6).

Tommy said that the danger of living this crucified life is to lose sight of God's grace. How have you dealt with this tension between working out your salvation day by day and living every moment by grace?

"Do not judge, or you too will be judged. For in the same way you judge others, you will be judged, and with the measure you use, it will be measured to you" (Matthew 7:1-2).

Many of us, as we seek out and walk the narrow path, become critical of those who walk the broader path. Oswald Chambers says that in the spiritual domain nothing is accomplished by criticism (*My Utmost for His Highest*, June 17th). How do you walk in the light that God has given you without using that light to judge others?

Part 3

To love at all is to be vulnerable.

Love anything, and your heart will certainly

be wrung and possibly be broken.

If you want to make sure of keeping it intact,

you must give your heart to no one,

not even to an animal.

Wrap it carefully round with hobbies and little luxuries;

avoid all entanglements;

lock it up safe in the casket or coffin of your selfishness.

But in that casket—safe, dark, motionless, airless—

it will change.

It will not be broken;

it will become unbreakable, impenetrable, irredeemable.

The alternative to tragedy, or at least the risk of tragedy,

is damnation.

The only place outside of Heaven

where you can be perfectly safe from all the dangers

and perturbations of love is Hell.

C. S. Lewis,
"The Four Loves"

Chapter 16
"Descending the Rope"

$\mathcal{T}$o choose to suffer

means that there is something wrong;

to choose God's will even if it means suffering

is a very different thing.

Oswald Chambers,
My Utmost for His Highest

The rhythm of the rain thumping on the skylights over my bed woke me. It was three a.m. My shoulders ached. My neck ached. My arms ached. As I rolled over to find a more comfortable position, my thoughts turned to Tommy. He could not roll over. He could not move his shoulders, his neck, or his arms to ease the tension or alleviate the pain. All at once, my aches and pains felt like time served for a misdemeanor compared to the hard time that Tommy was doing. I prayed for Tommy until I fell back asleep.

The following morning I ran through the pouring rain past the pink spirea that lay beaten down on the hostas. Several days of continuous rain had left the stone birdbath in the cottage garden spilling over with water. Shaking the rain off my shoulders and out of my hair as I stepped onto the front porch of Tommy's house, I couldn't help but notice anew the three rocks firmly planted in the garden amidst purple flowers. Each rock was chiseled with the name of a different virtue. The first was FAITH, the second HOPE, and the third LOVE. Faith, hope, and love, three enduring virtues, three sentinels against a life-taking disease. How appropriate that they should mark the entrance to Tommy's now dwindling world.

The shelves of books in Tommy's office that had so much been a part of Tommy's world and our conversations were no longer the backdrop for our meetings. Tommy no longer went to the office. Even the sun porch, where in the early fall he sat in his wheelchair meeting with congregates and friends, was no longer a part of Tommy's world. He no longer came downstairs to the sun porch.

Now confined to his bed and positioned on the side nearest the door,

Tommy smiled, rolling his eyes upward towards me in greeting as I entered his room. "It's hard not being able to talk clearly," he struggled. "Thoughts of healing tend to be somewhat dynamic. I'm always holding things in tension. I find myself doing two seemingly opposite things. One is preparing for and accepting my eventual death—it will come sooner or later, no matter what. At the same time I am holding onto the hope of doing something more in this life. When I think of my youngest child, Luke, and my wife, Sandy, there is a sense that I'm not finished. I don't know how to reconcile that. It is my relationships with Luke and Sandy that I feel are left unfinished. Ministry is another matter. God can use anyone for that."

I pulled the rocking chair up close to the bed so that I could see Tommy's eyes as he spoke. For a moment, his frail body looked like a crumpled piece of wrapping paper tossed among the pillows that propped him up. I shook the image out of my mind, focusing on Tommy's words.

Tommy continued, "Father and husband are different. I have this desire to finish that assignment—to ask for healing.

"I think faith is the key to receiving anything from God. I can't convince myself that my faith is any more special than another's faith, so I'm left putting this back into God's hands. It would be easier to simply accept my impending death than to remain in this tension. I'm expecting God to make Himself known in this matter. I think I will be greatly disappointed if He doesn't. It is hard to live with the tension and the mystery, but I know that it's the path to true spirituality.

"I have this image. I am standing on the edge of an abyss, looking down into an all-consuming darkness. I see myself holding this rope with one end tied around a rock and the other end tied around my waist. I firmly grasp the rope with both hands and begin lowering myself down over the precipice, descending into the darkness. As I inch down the cliff, the darkness becomes impenetrable. Nothing exists apart from my fear and my fists clenching into the rope. I become dizzy and disoriented, losing all sense of direction. When it feels as if all is lost and I am about to be annihilated by the blackness, my eyes adjust and a faint glimmer of light appears to be moving toward me. I realize that there is a lantern vaguely illuminating the walls of the cliff, revealing etchings left by those who have also gone this way. Some have only descended a few feet and then turned around and climbed back out. Others have obviously gone farther. As I continue the descent into the blackness, the lantern and the etchings become only a memory. I am alone, with only the piece of rope tied around my waist and clenched in my fists, unsure as to whether the piece of rope tied around me and held by me is still tied to the rock above. With fear and trembling I am descending into an incomprehensible Mystery, alone with the Alone. That's all I know for sure.

"I kind of like the rain," Tommy said, noticing that I had glanced at the window, the pulsating thumping of the rain momentarily distracting me from Tommy's words.

"What do you think about placing a challenge before God—asking Him for direction?" he continued. "I'm trying to be cautious. There is the fear that I am being presumptuous, but I'm prepared to accept whatever He puts before me. I just want to know what it is that God wants me to accept. From my vantage point, I see three options: either this is my time and He will come for me soon, or there will be some form of deliverance, or I am to be patient and wait in the mystery.

"I'm trying to discern the true nature of this test, and I am so aware that most of the world is suffering in some way—many in desperate situations. I don't want that awareness to deceive me into believing that I am too special on the one hand or inconsequential on the other. I want to see God as One who deals with each circumstance in a personal way, so that what happens for me does not hinge on what God is doing for someone else. For two and one-half years I have been in the same spot. I remember the story about the men who were waiting to die, and finally one says, 'Why are we sitting here waiting to die? Let's get up and do something.' I've needed these two and one-half years to learn about relinquishment, but I know there is something beyond relinquishment, and I am ready to move into that. This is a different space and I'm surprised by it. I know that I could not have gone further into this mystery without having first come down the path of relinquishment. (I think what comes next certainly must involve some kind of intervention from God. I know that it is some kind of resurrection, and I wonder how much my faith has to do with what kind of resurrection that will be? The final step down into this

159

mystery has to be one of grace—a gift from God."

$\mathcal{F}$or $\mathcal{R}$eflection

"My purpose is that they may be encouraged in heart and united in love, so that they may have the full riches of complete understanding, in order that they may know the mystery of God, namely, Christ, in whom are hidden all the treasures of wisdom and knowledge" (Colossians 2:2-3).

As Tommy traveled down the path of relinquishment, he found himself face to face with the mystery of God. What aspects of the nature of God remain a mystery for you?

"Search me, O God, and know my heart; test me and know my anxious thoughts. See if there is any offensive way in me, and lead me in the way everlasting" (Psalm 139:23-24).

What is it that God wants you to accept?

"...neither height nor depth, nor anything else in all creation, will be able to separate us from the love of God that is in Christ Jesus our Lord" (Romans 8:39).

How can we know experientially that nothing can separate us from the love of God unless we know hardship as well? How can we reach out to others who are traveling in the valley or wilderness places of life? Who is there in your life right now who needs a loving touch from you?

Chapter 17
"Elijah Must Go"

*W*hen "big" men go we are sad,

until we see that they are meant to go,

the one thing that remains

is looking in the face of God for ourselves.

Oswald Chambers,
My Utmost for His Highest

With pen and paper tucked under my sweater, I again ran through the pouring rain to Tommy's house. Tommy's room had now become a pleasant sanctuary from all the chaos of daily living and again on this occasion, a retreat from the chilling rain. The now familiar pieces of artwork, one by each of his children, still hung over his bed next to a photograph of his two daughters taken at his oldest daughter's wedding. There was a small poster on the dresser. On it, written in blue ink, were the words, "I only pray on days that end in 'Y.'" Everything in the room spoke of his focus on faith, his playful sense of humor, and his high regard for family—although I couldn't help but wonder if his family now felt cheated. Tommy's years had been given to and consumed by ministry. How does a wife or a child reconcile such loss, even for a good cause?

Tommy greeted me with his smiling eyes. "I now have a feeding tube to make things easier, but this feeding tube was a major setback. Eating took a lot of energy. This was supposed to be an outpatient procedure, but they had to keep me overnight. I don't think I was a good patient. I spent a miserable night in a terrible bed with the guy in the next bed also awake all night. They wouldn't release me until the doctor came the next morning. I was just hanging around. It was hard to be spiritual.

"My voice is stronger today, but when I'm in a crowd of more than two, I don't try to talk. It's extremely frustrating.

"I'm still shaping my understanding of how God works. I still believe that God is personally involved in my day-to-day existence, but it is difficult to figure it all out. It is difficult to maintain an eternal perspective. I'm constantly amazed at how much we are held by time."

Swallowing as he struggled to form each word, Tommy continued, "I am increasingly aware of the importance of having someone in our lives who gives us spiritual direction, someone who calls us to travel the higher road. Most of us live our lives without such mentors, meandering aimlessly, often going from church to church, in and out of relationships in our quest for such a person. The only alternative to being mentored is suffering. Suffering, pain in whatever form, seems to loosen our grip on the things of this world. If it doesn't, I don't know what will. All my preaching on letting go is ineffective compared to a good dose of pain or life's disappointments in any form. Even in suffering, though, we need someone who can help us extract meaning from our pain. I've been hard put to find such a person for myself. Most of my mentoring has come from books. I've been a student of books and life." This was not the first time that Tommy and I had talked about mentors. In September of 1997, after the media had bombarded the world with the shocking news of the premature death of Princess Diana of Wales, we had a conversation about mentors and idols. At that time, ALS had been Tommy's companion for less than two years, and he still had the strength and energy to converse about current events.

"It is safe to let our heroes be one hundred years old." Tommy had said. "What do you suppose the disciples saw in Christ as they walked through the dusty streets with him? They, too, were obviously looking for a hero. They had the same need that we all have: someone to lift them higher. Simon Peter said, 'Lord, to whom shall we go? You have the words of eternal life' (John 6:68). Jesus' words gave the 'Aha.' His life backed it up. His works—the miracles—authenticated everything that He said about Himself, so much so that the disciples knew that while they were with Him, they were in the presence of the Almighty God. Years later, as they sat down to write their memoirs, they must have reflected on how He had always pointed to the Father. The challenge for all of us is to be aware that what we truly long for is to connect to the heavenly Father. Our human heroes and heroines are just that, human. They are only signposts pointing to the One who is greater. If we remain unconscious of that fact, our heroes and heroines become larger than life, idols, and we begin to worship them. "I think it would be easy for a cynic to propose that Christianity was built around a hero or a heroine. Any good man's or good woman's life that ends in tragedy can become the basis for a system of religion.

"The intriguing question is, 'What's the difference between Christianity, built around the words and works of Jesus, and what in one hundred years could be built around the words and works of Diana; Martin Luther King, Jr.; Ghandi; or even John F. Kennedy?' We have to answer that question in an honest way. The answer has to be that Christ arose from the dead. The cross event is the only difference.

"Every generation seeks a hero or heroine of extraordinary quality to guide them along the higher road. It is a tragedy that so many fixate on the guide, and when that person is no longer there, they abandon the journey."

As I drove away from Tommy's house, the rhythmic humming and thumping of the windshield wipers against the spattering rain on the windows created a sound-barrier to the outside world, freeing my mind to process all the things that Tommy and I had talked about. I know that a great number of people, both within the church and the community at large, had been mentored by Tommy. For many, he had pointed the way to the higher road, the way of the cross. In the writing of this book, I, too, was being mentored by Tommy. How sad that the very gift he gave others, he had not found for himself.

Only a few weeks before, John Cernero, one of the pastors at Northview Christian Life, had talked about mentoring relationships in Scripture. He pointed to two in particular: the relationship between Moses and Joshua and the relationship between Elijah and Elisha. In both cases the hero had to go so that the one who followed would be able to look into the face of God for himself.

Joshua had been taught by Moses. Moses was his mentor. Before Moses died, Moses laid his hands on Joshua and "...Joshua son of Nun was filled with the spirit of wisdom... " (Deuteronomy 34:9).

"After the death of Moses...the Lord said to Joshua son of Nun, '...Moses my servant is dead....I will give you every place where you set your foot, as I promised Moses'" (Joshua 1:1-3).

The spirit of wisdom that was on Moses, Joshua's mentor and spiritual father, was now given to Joshua. The intimate bond, the "alongside" relationship of Joshua to Moses, prepared Joshua to look into the face of God for himself, to go forth and conquer the land.

Centuries later, a great prophet was raised up in Israel. Elijah, like Moses, was also a spiritual father and mentor, and all that God imparted to him was given to Elisha.

"As they were walking along and talking together, suddenly a chariot of fire and horses of fire appeared and separated the two of them, and Elijah went up to heaven in a whirlwind. Elisha saw this and cried out, 'My father! My father!'" (2 Kings 2:11-12*a*).

It was now left for Elisha to look into the face of God for himself. "He picked up the cloak that had fallen from Elijah and went back and stood on the bank of the Jordan. Then he took the cloak that had fallen from him and struck the water with it," just as he had seen Elijah do.

"'Where now is the Lord, the God of Elijah?' he asked. When he struck the water, it divided to the right and to the left, and he crossed over" (vs 13-14). The spirit of Elijah now rested on Elisha.

"It is not wrong to depend upon Elijah as long as God gives him to you," states Oswald Chambers, "but remember the time will come when he will have to go; when he stands no more to you as your guide and leader, because God does not intend he should. You say—'I cannot go on without Elijah.' God says you must."[1]

Both phrases, "After the death of Moses" and "he saw him no more," speak of God's providential will to take His servant home and to call the one who has been mentored, the one left behind, to begin to trust God for himself. I wonder if the time is soon to be for all of us who have been mentored by Tommy to begin to look into the face of God for ourselves.

For Reflection

"As they were walking along and talking together, suddenly a chariot of fire and horses of fire appeared and separated the two of them, and Elijah went up to heaven in a whirlwind. Elisha saw this and cried out, 'My father! My father! . . .'" (2 Kings 2:11-12a).

Tommy longed for a mentor. He said that the only alternative to being mentored is suffering, but even in suffering, we need someone who can help us extract meaning from our pain. Have you had a mentor, whether living or historical, who has helped you find meaning in a time of suffering?

Even a good mentor can keep us from looking into the face of God for ourselves. Has someone you loved or looked up to left you? Looking back, how has the loss of that person allowed you to look into the face of God for yourself?

Chapter 18
"Life in a Hermitage"

$\mathcal{W}$e imagine that we have to reach some end,
but that is not the nature of spiritual life.
The nature of spiritual life
is that we are certain in our uncertainty . . .
gracious uncertainty is the mark of the spiritual life.
To be certain of God
means that we are uncertain in all our ways.

Oswald Chambers,
My Utmost for His Highest

It was one of those mornings! Between my counseling and writing schedule, I often woke up as exhausted as when I went to bed. This morning was no exception. I opened the bread drawer and pulled out the sack of bread. There were only three pieces left—one of them was a heel. I had to make a quick decision. I could grab something for breakfast on my way to work or I could fix myself some toast and allow my husband to fend for himself. I decided to allow my husband to fend for himself. Whether coincidence or divine retribution for my selfishness, I'm not sure, but I was stuffing the last bite of toast into my mouth as I got into my car, and my car wouldn't start. I ran back into the house and begged my sixteen-year-old daughter, Charity Starr, to lend me her broken-down Honda so that I could get to the church on time for my first counseling session and later go to Tommy's house.

Going north on Keystone Avenue towards Carmel, a trucker passed yelling obscenities as he drove by. Being a middle-aged woman, I chalked it up to his having poor eyesight. It wasn't until I was walking out of the church with my last client that I gained some insight as to what that had actually been about. As we were walking through the parking lot, she pointed to a car in the far corner and said, "Did you see the bumper sticker on that car?" She was pointing to my daughter's beat-up Honda. There, plastered across the back of the car I had driven to church was a bumper sticker that read "PORN STAR." Although I learned later that PORN STAR is the name of a skateboard company, and that one of my daughter's friends thought that the PORN STAR bumper sticker would be a humorous addition to my daughter's broken-down Honda, I was not amused. In fact, I was red-hot!

Words that I rarely used were still running through my head when I arrived at Tommy's house. I stopped and prayed for the Lord to silence my thoughts and direct me so that I could wholly enter into the task at hand. I remembered something Tommy had said to me a few months ago, "The grace that God will have to give me to die is the same grace that you need to live." With that in mind, I walked up the drive and began to enter Tommy's world.

Tommy's world had shrunk to the size of a pea. Baskets of yellow and pink fresh flowers perched on the front porch, a new arrangement of the furniture in his living room, quips and family photos added to the refrigerator door—all the places and things of Tommy's life, even those in his own home, were becoming a memory. His world, like his body, had shriveled up. Tommy, however, received the small space that he now occupied as a hermitage and not a prison.

"I'm waiting and watching to see how this unfolds. It's pretty much in God's hands. I've done most of what I have to do," Tommy began. "My greatest pleasure is meditating on the Lord. Scripture continues to engulf me." Tommy raised his eyebrows. "I'm at the end of my strength. Each time I say that, though, I find more strength, more letting go. I've lost most of my speech. If I were ever to get my speech back, I would have much to say."

Watching Tommy as he, with great effort, shaped his facial muscles in order to form words, I couldn't help but notice how frail he now looked. His face was like that of a very old man. His lips were dry and peeling. Even though the warm June air had rolled through the open window and enveloped him, he was dressed in a long-sleeved T-shirt and sweatpants. Tommy paused for a moment and turned his gaze towards me as if he had just read my mind. "Is it hard for you to see me like this?" he asked.

"No. Not at all. I look forward to each visit with you," I replied, fumbling for words. "Tommy, are you able to sleep?" I asked, shifting the focus of the conversation back to Tommy.

"At night I can only sleep for an hour at a time, then I have to move. I hate waking Sandy to move me, but that's the way it is. Sometimes I lie here too long because I don't want to wake her. The pain gets excruciating when I lie too long in one position. I haven't been comfortable in over a year. Sometimes I'm just less uncomfortable."

With a grimace-smile, Tommy continued. "I can sit in my chair for about fifteen minutes and then I begin to struggle. I can't talk at all when I'm sitting up in the chair. The last time that I went to church, people came up and asked me questions. I couldn't respond with words, so I just smiled to let them know I love them.

"I'm so pleased by the church and staff. Last night I think you would have been proud of them. There was a meeting where the church talked about what was to happen next. Everyone was so supportive.

"I think we have a chance to create something extraordinary, something resembling the true body of the Lord. If the Lord decided to heal me, I know that we could never go back to where we were before. The church has moved light years ahead of that time. I like the way the people are holding all these things in tension, living in uncertainty. It's what I taught for so long. We are entering the mystery of God.

"I think if there were to be a miracle, it would have to be in that environment. The whole church has to let go of me just as I have to let go of all of them. I am convinced that any true miracle can only occur in the environment of complete surrender. It is a difficult path to walk. I want to go that way." Tommy paused and swallowed several times. Then he continued. "The Lord has impressed on me the idea of being pure in heart."

I wanted to stop Tommy and ask, "As a man standing on the bridge, what do you mean by pure in heart?" but I didn't want to interrupt the flow of his thoughts and perhaps miss something else that he really needed to say.

"Many years ago when I was in excellent health, I preached a sermon on faith. Last year, before my health deteriorated to what it is today, I improved on that sermon and preached it again. I would love for the Lord to give me another chance to preach that sermon, only this time from the other side. I would like to know how it feels from all three vantage points. That's the beauty of God's word; it has the power to speak to us no matter where we are on our journey."

Tommy scrunched his eyebrows together and smiled. "I'm stretching." The stretch would have gone unnoticed except for a slight movement with his left foot.

"I decided early on that this is a spiritual journey. Others take different roads, but for me, it has to be spiritual from beginning to end. I think that my whole life has prepared me for this time. In some sense that is all that life is, a preparation for death. It is comfortable to look back and see how God has prepared and given meaning to everything that has gone before. It is not always easy to apprehend that meaning." Tommy stopped and gulped. It now took tremendous energy for Tommy to continue, but he still had more to say. "There are always at least two possible things that could be going on. One is that I am in the process of dying and God is preparing me to cross the bridge to the next life. The other is that he has another purpose for my life. I'm caught in a quandary. I am uncertain of God's intent, but I am certain of God.

"In the next month or so, I believe God will show me what he has for me."

As I climbed back into my daughter's broken-down Honda—with all its offensiveness—I pondered the ups and downs, turbulence, chaos, unpredictability, and often overwhelmingness of my world. Then I thought about the pea-sized world that Tommy now occupied. The grace that God will give me to live is the same grace that God will give Tommy to die.

Later that afternoon my friend Susan picked me up, and we drove to South Bend, Indiana, for a two-day conference. In the middle of the night I awoke overwhelmed with a feeling of sadness. "Is it hard for you to see me like this?" Tommy had asked me. As a counselor, my effectiveness depends on my ability to empathize with others while distancing myself from their pain. For the first time since we had begun collaborating on this book, Tommy was not the pastor, the mentor, or the subject of a book, but he was "Tommy," a person I had come to love, appreciate, and care for deeply. It was unsettling to feel so vulnerable.

The words of C. S. Lewis, "Love anything and your heart will certainly be wrung and possibly broken," had always been for someone else. I didn't like the way they fit when I put them on.

$\mathcal{F}$or $\mathcal{R}$eflection

"And without faith it is impossible to please God, because anyone who comes to him must believe that he exists and that he rewards those who earnestly seek him" (Hebrews 11:6).

Tommy said that if the Lord decided to heal him, the church could never go back to where it was before. How do you think your church would change if God were to do a similar miracle?

As Tommy's body deteriorated and God seemingly remained silent, his faith grew. Have you encountered a situation where your faith has grown even though God remained silent?

What characterizes faith in the face of seemingly unanswered prayer?

Chapter 19
"A Sequestered Path"

*F*aith never knows where it is being led,

but it loves and knows the One Who is leading.

Oswald Chambers,
My Utmost for His Highest

As always, the front door stood ajar, welcoming me into Tommy and Sandy's house. When I walked to the kitchen to get a cup of coffee, I could hear the water from the sprinklers hitting the kitchen window over the sink. Its sound reminded me that this was the first time in several weeks that I had visited Tommy when it was not raining. My eyes caught the basket of glazed fruit and ivy on the lace doily on the old oak table in the kitchen. I made a mental note that a variation of that arrangement would be attractive on my own kitchen table. Upstairs Tommy lay curled on his bed, his elbow bent under him propping up his body and a pillow between his legs. Even after all of these months, his sparkling brown eyes and his infectious smile never failed to surprise me. His body continued to wither away, and yet the undaunted joy of his soul emanated from his eyes, and his high regard for others was always present in his smile. I now sat close to him on the bed in order to read his lips. His weakening voice, like the sound of the birds in a tree outside his bedroom window, faded in and out.

"Tommy, it's always good to see you. How are you doing today?" I asked.

Tommy grimaced slightly, as he now did frequently, silently expressing his uncomfortableness. "I have lots of time to pray, but I'm upset at myself because my own suffering gets in the way. I'm trying to use this time to pray for others, but it's hard to do.

"I'm amazed that I have come this far and am still functioning. I wonder how much longer we can do this. Some things are scary—like taking a shower. If I ever fall off my chair in the shower, it's all over."

I leaned closer to his crumpled body, sensing that he had something important to say.

"I want to trust God completely," Tommy whispered, "but that's easy to say and hard to do. Coming to that place is a gift only God can give me. I can't do it on my own. Being in a place where I have almost no control allows me to see how impossible it would be for me to do it on my own. I have always lived with the illusion of control. Much of this process is coming to grips with disillusionment. When someone says, 'I'm disillusioned,' what they really mean is, 'I'm coming to grips with the way things really are.' Christ moves us out of our illusions into reality. The final place in this journey of trust is ultimately a gift from God." Tommy closed his eyes for a moment. "That shouldn't have surprised me," he added. "Even now I grasp for control.

"I still enjoy people who have come to visit me all along, but it is increasingly difficult to engage them in conversation. I don't mind people reading to me. New people are hard to bring up to speed. Most of them start crying when they see me. I do enjoy new people, but it's more difficult now.

"It is difficult for me to accept death when I still have so much that I want to say, but death is closer. When there is a great deal of pain, I feel trapped and fight anxiety and panic. I often feel that way when people come by for small talk. It drives me crazy. I can't escape. There's nothing worse than being trapped by small talk and not being able to respond or escape. Time is so short. I want people to say what's on their hearts. I know small talk is their way of connecting when they don't know what to say, but it's difficult for me."

The sound of Tommy's voice creaked as he began to talk about hope. "I don't want to lose hope. Somehow, our hope has to stretch from here to eternity." Tommy turned his eyes towards the nightstand by the bed, as if to motion to me to get something from there. "I'm reading *The Cloister Walk*."

I walked around to the nightstand and picked up the book by Kathleen Norris. *The Cloister Walk* is a diary of the years that Kathleen Norris who, as a Protestant, a poet, a married woman, and a layperson, lived a monastic life as a Benedictine. She states that, "Gradually my perspective on time had changed. In our culture, time can seem like an enemy: it chews us up and spits us out with appalling ease. But the monastic perspective welcomes time as a gift from God, and seeks to put it to good use rather than allowing us to be used up by it."[1] Tommy was now attempting to view time from this strange perspective. His body no longer moved through time as it once had. The squares on his daily planner were no longer distinct one from another. Tommy was now cradled in a pocket of time where only these three things remained: faith, hope, and love. *The Cloister Walk* was a welcome mentor, a royal road map for traveling this last mile in the treacherous terrain of his human experience to the place where time will be no more.

Many times during his years of ministry, Tommy had prayed:

> Oh Lord,
> I pray that when the time of testing comes into my life, that you may find that the faith that I have offered to you in the good times is able to stand steady and secure, even in the dark times. When my feelings betray me, when my thoughts will no longer take me to a place of hope, may you find in me the will and the desire to love you and stay true to you no matter what.

What had begun as a trial of faith and a test of hope had now become a dialogue with mystery, a faith that transcends the darkness, a hope that stretches to eternity, and ultimately the knowledge of the perfect and extravagant love of God.

For Reflection

"I know what it is to be in need, and I know what it is to have plenty. I have learned the secret of being content in any and every situation, whether well fed or hungry, whether living in plenty or in want" (Philippians 4:12).

Tommy had often prayed that the faith he had offered to God during the good times would also stand steady and secure in the dark times. We all go through good times and dark times. How have you experienced faith in a dark time?

Do you feel closer to God when times are good or when times are dark? Why?

Chapter 20
"The Deafening Silence"

Song birds are taught to sing in the dark,
and we are put into the shadow of God's hand
until we learn to hear Him.

Oswald Chambers,
My Utmost for His Highest

The chapters of Tommy's life that were once measured out in years were now moments cupped in the hands of God. It was July 9th, 1998.

For the first two years Tommy had courageously fought the whirling winds of ALS. In the beginning, the gray clouds that had crawled across his internal landscape had frightened him. He girded himself with the whole armor of God and continued down the steep path. He was a man of faith. He was a man who trusted God in all things. But now the clouds had turned an ominous black. Tommy had entered the mysterious darkness of God's deafening silence.

The scent of fresh flowers that greeted me as I entered the house gave way to the smell of liniment at the threshold to Tommy's room. The physical distance that I had always kept out of respect for his personal space no longer seemed relevant. I leaned over on the bed up close to Tommy. I wanted to be sure that I could read his lips. With great strain Tommy began to speak.

"…uncomfortable. I can't change positions. It's the worst pain— unrelenting. Nothing I can do. So much depends on how I feel physically. Some days are torturous—everything closes in on me. I feel panic in those moments. The mental anguish is worse than the physical pain. When I am left in discomfort, the pain drowns out everything, and I can't stay present with people. I'm caught in that I don't want to complain, but I don't want to lie either. Usually I say nothing. I'm not sailing through this. It wears thin after a while."

Tommy stopped for a moment, signaling a shift. "God seems to be hiding Himself. It is not easy to accept things that have no answers. I am convinced that it is impossible for me to move through this in my natural faith. Others cannot understand what this is like. It's too much to ask. I never understood before. Now I'm totally alone in this place of deafening silence. People want to help me, but they cannot come with me on this part of the journey. I believe that the light will come, but I can't say for sure. That's what faith is all about.

"There's so much that I want to say, but it stays bottled up inside of me." With a slight pursed smile, Tommy added, "For someone as verbal as I am, it's enough to drive me nuts.

"I know that sometimes I drive Sandy nuts, because I need so much help—for almost everything now. It's amazing that she is able to stay positive most of the time. I'm sure she can't allow herself to feel any other way right now.

"We've been married for thirty-one years. It has been quite easy to stay married to her for that long."

It was only on rare occasions during our times together that Tommy would digress and share personal information. As a counselor, I know that people who always focus on others or God are very private people. Even in the writing of this book, it has been my intent to respect that privacy, but I couldn't help but savor this uncommon moment.

"I think a mistake that I am making is trying to figure God out," Tommy continued from a different train of thought. "It is the one thing that I will never be able to do—a frightening place to be. My model of God does not fit in this place. It is a mystery. The Bible is a book of revelation that makes God known. I am in a place of darkness where I cannot sing—I cannot see God. I am waiting for a supernatural gift of faith in order to be able to remain here. I am so tired, but I think I am supposed to abide here for some reason. I'm trying not to check out on life. That's not an option for me. I know that there are many people who endure this kind of pain indefinitely. I'm trying to remember that I'm not the only one who has to remain in this place of mystery and unknowing. I'm trying not to feel sorry for myself."

I knew that Tommy tired easily, so I gathered my purse and papers and excused myself. The rest would come more easily at another time.

On the ride home I thought about an incident that we had talked about a little more than a year ago. Someone had come to Tommy with what she believed to be a message from God. Like Tommy, she too had been drawn to the writings of Oswald Chambers. The word God had given to this person for Tommy came through the daily reading of *My Utmost for His Highest*. October eleventh reads:

> ...God's silences are His answers....God will give you the blessings you ask if you will not go any further without them...As long as you have the idea that God will bless you in answer to prayer, He will do it, but He will never give you the grace of silence. If Jesus Christ is bringing you into the understanding that prayer is for the glorifying of His Father, He will give you the first sign of His intimacy—silence.[1]

That very morning at breakfast Tommy had said to Sandy that he had this sense that God was going to speak to him. The irony was that God spoke to him by graciously breaking the silence to give him the assurance that His silence was pregnant with meaning. Tommy, too, had to pause and take in the words of Oswald Chambers, "God will give you the blessings you ask if you will not go any further without them."

When we first talked about this incident and God's gracious silence as his answer, Tommy had said, "I want an answer, and I am tempted to go no further, but therein lies the test. Can God trust me with a big silence? I want the answer to be 'Yes,' but I also want the answer to be 'No.'"

Over this past year, even as Tommy's health crumbled, I had seen him cling to these words of Oswald Chambers, pressing into the silence of God. Tommy, a man of answers, was now embracing the God of all answers. Tommy, a man of words, had entered the intimacy of God's deafening silence—a place without words.

For Reflection

"God will give you the blessings you ask if you will not go any further without them." Oswald Chambers says. How have the blessings of God kept you from seeking a more intimate relationship with God?

"Let him sit alone in silence, for the LORD has laid it on him.
Let him bury his face in the dust—there may yet be hope.
Let him offer his cheek to one who would strike him, and let him be filled with disgrace.
For men are not cast off by the Lord forever.
Though he brings grief, he will show compassion, so great is his unfailing love.
For he does not willingly bring affliction or grief to the children of men" (Lamentations 3:28-33).

Have you, too, experienced a time of silence from God? At times, the community of grace supports us. At other times we, like Tommy, must press into that silence for ourselves in absolute submission. What gives us strength in these times?

Chapter 21
"An Unkind Friend"

There are times . . . when God cannot lift

the darkness from you, but trust Him.

God will appear like an unkind friend, but He is not;

He will appear like an unnatural Father, but He is not;

He will appear like an unjust judge, but He is not.

Oswald Chambers,
My Utmost for His Highest

The headlines in the morning paper read, "Two Hundred Feared Dead in Bombing." My eyes moved down the page, begging to be distracted. I flipped through the paper until I arrived at the entertainment page. Momentarily I could dismiss the fact that, like Tommy, I, too, was terminally ill and on a voyage destined for death. Tommy's terminal illness is incurable and irreversible. The illness of my human condition is also incurable and irreversible. There is one difference, though. Tommy's ship was reprogrammed to arrive at his destination in two, or maybe three years. (He journeys by faith, conscious of his destination, deliberately living every moment of every day, feeling all of the emotions of dying while he is still alive.) I, like so many others, disguise my dying body. I may minimize that fact, quipping that I don't use fancy attire, face-lifts, or Clairol to color my graying hair, but in truth, I don't want to believe that I am in the process of dying. I, like so many others, deny my fear of dying by working longer hours. Others buy bigger houses and run more laps— as if they could outrun time and cheat death. But eventually time, our ever-present companion, ceases to befriend us, and like Tommy we, too, will be left with all our God questions crumpled in a heap at the foot of death's bed, begging to be answered. Even our pumped-up prayers cannot stay the execution of life as we know it if God has purposed otherwise.

Abraham Schmitt in *Dialogue with Death* states that as long as "we are not diagnosed terminally ill, we dilute our present with as much of the past as we can regurgitate and as much of the future as we can fantasize."[1] Tommy's future resides in his hope in the next life, and his past will soon be only what is left in the memories of those who knew him.

Hanging baskets of pink geraniums greeted me as I arrived at Tommy's front door. An old school desk with more geraniums sat in the corner of the porch next to a pot of white daisies. Black-eyed Susans smiled from along a split rail fence. One would hardly imagine that death was stalking at the back door.

I let myself in and went up the stairs to Tommy's bedroom. Tommy's bright brown eyes seemed larger against his shriveling body. The crooked fingers of his left hand cupped his right hand. He appeared much weaker. It was the first time I had seen him when he was not clean-shaven.

"It is a most difficult time, because it is no longer possible to sense God's presence in the ways I have always been accustomed to," Tommy said, no longer wasting words. "It is very hard to see God as a kind friend. I can't explain it. I don't have the ability to move forward on my own. Faith is more . . . to have . . . . Pray for my family." For the first time, I couldn't understand all of his words or read his lips. Feeling his frustration increased my anxiety. I wanted to hear his every word. His words were increasingly important to me. He had something to say that few others had opportunity to put into words. I didn't want to miss important words. In hopes of alleviating my anxiety, I reverted to small talk. I asked him if as many people as before still made the pilgrimage to his bedside.

"They come, but it is often more confusing....I don't ever want to believe that God is not able to heal me." I knew that Tommy was referring to those who came to pray for his healing. "At the same time, I want to embrace His plan, regardless of what that is," Tommy said, swallowing after each word.

"I'm in much discomfort. The real pain is my mental state. I'm fully knowledgeable of—I'm aware of the pain...pain that I'm causing...I'm so dependent on others for everything. To need others is hard. This is a most cruel disease." Tommy closed his eyes for a moment.

Even though his breathing seemed more labored, he continued, "It's time for the church to seek another pastor. It's so hard. I'm not coming back." I knew that letting go of control, surrendering his will, and submitting to God's purposes and not his own were all summed up in this one statement. Tommy had plunged the knife into his Isaac.

"Tommy, what's left to let go of?" I asked, not knowing how to re-

198

spond to what had to be a painful but profound realization.

For the first time since I walked into the room, Tommy grinned. "Not much, but I'm sure there's always something.

"I don't feel like a superhero. I've never been more aware of my weakness. Grace is what I'm counting on. I almost cringe…"

Tommy's voice trailed off and I began missing words.

"I'm so empty." Tommy shut his eyes; his breathing even more labored than before. "I think that all that I am is one person who tried to do his best. I am so aware of my need for rest."

I walked out the front door past the hanging baskets of pink geraniums into the warm sunshine. A gray cloud of sadness settled over my heart, for I had just seen the dreadful emptiness that engulfs the dying just before they are about to be called home. And yet my own grief was mixed with joy, knowing that the overwhelming emptiness is the same emptiness that Henri J. M. Nouwen calls "holy emptiness," one into which God the Father will pour His eternal peace and perfect love, welcoming His beloved home.

For Reflection

"It is better to go to a house of mourning than to go to a house of feasting, for death is the destiny of every man; the living should take this to heart" (Ecclesiastes 7:20).

Like Tommy, we too are terminally ill and on a voyage destined for death. How do you deny the eventuality of death?

How would consciously and deliberately feeling all the emotions of dying, while still alive, change the way you live?

"'Where, O death, is your victory? Where, O death, is your sting?'
The sting of death is sin, and the power of sin is the law.
But thanks be to God! He gives us the victory through our Lord Jesus Christ.
Therefore, my dear brothers, stand firm. Let nothing move you. Always give yourselves fully to the work of the Lord, because you know that your labor in the Lord is not in vain" (1 Corinthians 15:55-58).

Have you also come to the point where you will "embrace His plan, regardless of what that is"?

Do you know what the Isaac is in your life?

Chapter 22
"Parting Words"

*G*od's way is always the way of suffering . . .

We never realize at the time

what God is putting us through;

we go through it more or less misunderstanding;

then we come to a luminous place . . .

Oswald Chambers,
My Utmost for His Highest

For a moment, I gazed out the open window. It was a pink, bright day with cumulus clouds rolling across an azure blue sky, the kind of day that pleasant memories from childhood are made of. I walked over to the bed and sat down. Even though Tommy's shrunken body was dwarfed by the queen-sized bed, his eyes gave mass and substance to his presence.

"I…can't…talk," Tommy said, gulping for air between each word. I was ready to sit with his silence, with only the sound of a mower in the background, when Tommy began again. "I…have…learned…to move beyond…the…emptiness. I…have…learned…to embrace it. This…is… part of the…journey. It…is the place…where almost… everything else… is…gone."

Tommy paused, measuring every word. "I can't put…my…thoughts into long…sentences…"

As the lawn mower came back around under the open window, the roar of the mower engulfed the fragmented whisper from Tommy's lips, stealing precious words. Tommy was frustrated at not being able to speak. I was frustrated at not being able to hear.

We waited for another pass of the lawn mower. I read to him from *The Cloister Walk*.

Unsettled by the intrusion from outside, I lost my focus and reverted to my natural random style of conversation. On the previous Monday, Tommy's daughter Sarah had returned to college. It had been an emotionally wrenching time for him. I asked Tommy how he was doing with all that now. "I couldn't…tell her…my…feelings," he said with a smile turning up the corners of his eyebrows.

As the sound of the lawn mower faded, Tommy returned to the

previous topic. He no longer had the stamina to repeat even one word. Slowly and deliberately he began, enunciating every syllable. "I'm...learning...to...embrace...the...darkness." I moved closer, waiting for him to continue. "It...is...a...place...of...revelation. I...wish...I...could...explain...it." His face was no longer contorted from the months of struggle. The only scrimmage left was the fight to force his lips and throat muscles to form words. "It's...an...awesome...place," Tommy said as he closed his eyes. "It's...probably... right...for...me...not...to...be...able...to...put...this...in...words."

I touched Tommy on the shoulder as we said goodbye. I was ready to go write a book. Tommy was ready to go home.

$\mathcal{F}$or $\mathcal{R}$eflection

"Precious in the sight of the Lord is the death of his saints." (Psalm 116:15).

"Then the eyes of those who see will no longer be closed, and the ears of those who hear will listen.
The mind of the rash will know and understand, and the stammering tongue will be fluent and clear" (Isaiah 32:3,4).

"So will it be with the resurrection of the dead. The body that is sown is perishable, it is raised imperishable; it is sown in dishonor, it is raised in glory; it is sown in weakness, it is raised in power; it is sown a natural body, it is raised a spiritual body" (1 Corinthians 15:42-44).

Tommy's hope was not based on his being a good man but rather on his relationship with Jesus, who Himself became the Doorway to eternal life. Do you know the One who gives us hope? Do you know Him personally?

Tommy's last words to the author are food for thought for all of us. "I'm learning to embrace the darkness. It is a place of revelation. I wish I could explain it. It's an awesome place. It's probably right for me not to be able to put this in words." How do these words personally affect your sense who God is?

Has the reading of this book affected your view of how God is working in your life?

"Now to him who is able to do immeasurably more than all we ask or imagine, according to his power that is at work within us, to him be glory in the church and in Christ Jesus throughout all generations, for ever and ever! Amen" (Ephesians 3:20,21).

Chapter 23
"The Storm"

*O*ften even love itself has to wait in pain and tears

for the blessing of fuller communion.

Oswald Chambers,
My Utmost for His Highest

In the cupped hands of God's silence, the storm came. First, darkness rolled across the painted sky, blotting out the yellow sun. The call came on Wednesday. Tommy Paino had turned in his ticket and entered heaven's gates before the beginning of the new day.

Like a thick goose down comforter the first snow storm of the new year blanketed the earth. Blowing snow turned to freezing rain, ice, and then more snow. In the last hours, it began to snow anew as all our prayers lay at the foot of the cross. Even God did not spare his own Son.

"And Flights of Angels Sing Thee to Thy Rest." It was over.

In the aftermath of the storm, the fresh snow settles over the gray mist of grief, calming and brightening the new day. Broken hearts begin to heal. All that remains is faith, hope, and love in the hearts of those who were changed by knowing Tommy, reminding us of the power of the storm and of the power of the God who quieted the storm.

In loving memory
Thomas Paino III
Presented to the world
February 5, 1946
Present with the Lord
January 5th, 1999
Welcome Home, Tommy!

Epilogue

They came from all over the country. A few flew in from other parts of the world. The snow, the ice, and the bitter cold did not deter them from gathering at the church Tommy loved. For hours they filed past the casket, greeting, hugging, remembering, and reminiscing. Grieving the loss of a good man, or at least a man who desired goodness, ultimately becomes a celebration. Tommy's death, like his life, became a celebration of all that is good, all that is true, and all that is worthy.

It was at the memorial service that Tommy's non-pastor brother, Troy, reminded us of the healing power of laughter and celebration.

"I don't know whether you realize this, but Tommy did us a favor," Troy began, "because as I positioned myself behind this pulpit, hell officially froze over. I have always looked to Tommy as my hero. I was the youngest brother, and in my eyes Tommy could do no wrong, but I have long since grown up and can now view Tommy from a very different perspective. Tommy was and is my hero, not because he was perfect—nor was he a comic book hero who had superhuman strength and could do no wrong—but because he was so human. He was fallible. In fact, sometimes amazingly so...

"Some years ago, our families took a vacation to Disney World. On one particularly hot day—one of those eggs-sizzling-on-the-pavement days, Tommy decided that he and I would go running. He assured me that what he had in mind was only a three- or four-mile run. Now keep in mind that in our family Tommy has always been the unquestionable leader. In fact, I would have followed Tommy off the Golden Gate Bridge if he had assured me that it would be fun. Despite the fact that only minutes before we had each indulged in a Big Mac meal at a nearby McDonald's, and despite the fact that he had no real course in mind, Tommy plopped his blue baseball cap on top of his bald head. I dutifully followed him out the door. After about twenty-five minutes of running under the scorching Florida sun, it became abundantly clear to me that Tommy had no idea where we were or where we were going. There we were, jogging down a busy Orlando street in the proximity of Disney World. The heat index was 100 degrees, the humidity 99 percent, and we were sprinting along with a couple of Big Macs weighing heavily on our stomachs.

"In hindsight, the prudent thing to do would have been to turn around, retrace our run, and call it a day. That, of course, would have meant a fifty-minute run, longer than either of us were willing to consider under the then present circumstances. Tommy looked at me and said, 'I know a quicker way back to the hotel. Just follow me.' Although a bit dubious, what other choice did I have but to dutifully follow him? He immediately headed down an entrance ramp onto Interstate 4. So picture this: two fools, by this time sick to their stomachs, running down a Florida interstate under the scorching sun—supposedly for their health.

"If Tommy were telling you this story, he would have wanted you to leave this service with at least one lesson. Here it is: Distances, while driving 65 miles per hour on interstates, seem shorter than while jogging along those same interstates under a hot Florida sun.

"We kept running. The exit to our hotel was nowhere in sight. All at once, Tommy veers off the shoulder of the interstate and disappears into a thicket of shrubbery. 'Tommy, are you okay?' I asked. No response. 'Tommy, can I do anything?' Again, no response.

"Five minutes later he emerges without his blue ball cap, his bald head gleaming under the hot Florida sun, and utters these respectful words. 'It was a good hat, a faithful hat, but more importantly, it was a soft hat.' I would like to say that the five miles we still had to run were filled with laughter, but the laughter came later. Keep in mind that, unlike Tommy, I still had that Big Mac weighing heavily on my stomach.

"Tommy had fun. He was fully human, but when he was diagnosed with ALS, he accepted his suffering for Christ's sake. I do not want to forget the last three and one-half years of Tommy's life, but I also want to remember all of the moments of fun and celebration that I shared with my brother. Tommy, thank you for your life."

Tommy Paino, III

Notes

Chapter Inscriptions

All chapter inscriptions are taken from *My Utmost for His Highest* by Oswald Chambers. (Westwood, New Jersey: Barbour and Company, 1963).

Chapter 1 – November 11
Chapter 2 – January 13
Chapter 3 – September 19
Chapter 4 – October 23
Chapter 5 – September 13
Chapter 6 – January 13
Chapter 7 – December 15
Chapter 8 – November 7
Chapter 9 – August 29
Chapter 10 – December 10
Chapter 11 – July 17
Chapter 12 – December 9
Chapter 13 – August 6
Chapter 14 – February 18
Chapter 15 – July 22
Chapter 16 – August 10
Chapter 17 – April 22
Chapter 18 – April 29
Chapter 19 – March 19
Chapter 20 – February 14
Chapter 21 – July 16
Chapter 22 – November 25
Chapter 23 – September 12

Part I

From "Who Am I?". Excerpted with the permission of Simon & Schuster from *Letters & Papers from Prison*, Revised, Enlarged Edition by Dietrich Bonhoeffer, translated by Reginald Fuller, Frank Clark et al. Copyright © 1953, 1967, 1971 by SCM Press, Ltd.

Chapter 3: "I Have Learned"
1. H. Jackson Brown, Jr. *Live and Learn and Pass It On* (Nashville: Rutledge Hill Press, 1992), 13, 14, 25, 28, 33, 142.

Chapter 4: The Potter's House
1. Philip Keller. "The Potter's House," an unidentified pamphlet.
2. G. C. Stebbins. "Have Thine Own Way, Lord" (Hope Publishing Co. 1935).

Chapter 5: Of Monks and Fruitcakes
1. Jonetta Hendel. "Absolute Surrender," unpublished poem used by permission.

Chapter 6: Am I Alone?
1. Henri J. M. Nouwen. *The Return of the Prodigal Son* (New York: Doubleday, 1992), 47.

Part II

Christini Rossetti. "A Better Resurrection," *Poems and Prose* (Rutland, Vermont: Orion, 1998), 52-53.

Chapter 8: "The Remembering One"
1. Larry Crabb. *The Silence of Adam* (Grand Rapids, Michigan: Zondervan, 1955), 79.
2. For an in-depth study of these six traditions, refer to Richard J. Foster. *Streams of Living Water* (San Francisco: HarperCollins, 1998).

Chapter 9: Undaunted Courage
1. Stephen E. Ambrose. *Undaunted Courage* (New York: Simon & Schuster, 1997).
2. T. S. Eliot. "Little Gidding" from *Four Quartets, Collected Poems 1909-1962* (New York: Harcourt Brace & Co., 1991), 208.

Chapter 12: "Beckoning to the Bridge"
1. Mitch Albom. *Tuesdays with Morrie* (New York: Doubleday, 1997), 9-10, 32-33.
2. Mrs. E. Prentiss. *Stepping Heavenward* (Uhrichville, Ohio: Barbour and Company, 1998), 315-316.

Chapter 14: "Trembling on Holy Ground"
1. Mercy/Vineyard Publishing. All rights reserved. Used by permission.

Chapter 15: "Good Friday"
1. Gerald Sittsler. *A Grace Disguised* (Grand Rapids, Michigan: Zondervan, 1996), 18.
2. Paula D'Arcy. *Gift of the Red Bird* (New York: Crossroad Publishing Company, 1998), 31.

Part III
C. S. Lewis, *The Four Loves* (New York: Harcourt Brace Jovanovich, 1960), 169.

Chapter 17: "Elijah Must Go"
1. Oswald Chambers. *My Utmost for His Highest* (Westwood, New Jersey: Barbour and Company, 1963), August 11th.

Chapter 19: "A Sequestered Path"
1. Kathleen Norris. *The Cloister Walk* (New York: Riverhead Books, 1997), *xix.*

Chapter 20: "The Deafening Silence"
1. Oswald Chambers, *My Utmost for His Highest* (Westwood, New Jersey: Barbour and Company, 1963), October 11th.

Chapter 21: "An Unkind Friend"
1. Abraham Schmitt. *Dialogue with Death* (Harrisonburg, Virginia: Choice Books, 1976), 112.

Works Cited

Albom, Mitch. *Tuesdays with Morrie.* New York: Doubleday, 1997.

Ambrose, Stephen E. *Undaunted Courage.* New York: Simon & Schuster, 1997.

Brown, Jr., Jackson H., ed. *Live and Learn and Pass it On.* Nashville: Rutledge Hill Press, 1992.

Chambers, Oswald. *My Utmost for His Highest.* Westwood, New Jersey: Barbour and Company, 1963.

Crabb, Larry. *The Silence of Adam.* Grand Rapids: Zondervan, 1955.

D'Arcy, Paula. *Gift of the Red Bird: A Spiritual Encounter.* New York: Crossroad Publishing Company, 1998.

Foster, Richard J. *Streams of Living Water.* San Francisco: HarperCollins, 1998.

Keller, Philip. "The Potter's House."

Norris, Kathleen. *The Cloister Walk.* New York: Riverhead Books, 1997.

Nouwen, Henri J. M. *The Return of the Prodigal Son.* New York: Doubleday, 1992.

Prentiss, Elizabeth. *Stepping Heavenward.* Uhrichville, Ohio: Barbour and Company, 1998.

Schmitt, Abraham. *Dialogue with Death.* Harrisonburg, Virginia: Choice Books, 1976.

Sittser, Gerald L. *A Grace Disguised.* Grand Rapids: Zondervan, 1996.